## Sussex

Edited by Jenni Bannister

First published in Great Britain in 2010 by

Remus House
Coltsfoot Drive
Peterborough
PE2 9JX
Telephone: 01733 890066
Website: www.youngwriters.co.uk

All Rights Reserved
Book Design by Spencer Hart
© Copyright Contributors 2009
SB ISBN 978-1-84924-789-4

# Foreword

At Young Writers our defining aim is to promote an enjoyment of reading and writing amongst children and young adults. By giving aspiring poets the opportunity to see their work in print, their love of the written word as well as confidence in their own abilities has the chance to blossom.

Our latest competition Poetry Explorers was designed to introduce primary school children to the wonders of creative expression. They were given free reign to write on any theme and in any style, thus encouraging them to use and explore a variety of different poetic forms.

We are proud to present the resulting collection of regional anthologies which are an excellent showcase of young writing talent. With such a diverse range of entries received, the selection process was difficult yet very rewarding. From comical rhymes to poignant verses, there is plenty to entertain and inspire within these pages. We hope you agree that this collection bursting with imagination is one to treasure.

# Contents

## All Saints CE Primary School
Jamila Cope (10) ................................. 1
Benjamin Bishop (11) ......................... 1
Jade Ennion (10) ................................ 2
Adele Wilson (11) ............................... 2
Jack Crompton (10) ............................ 3
Arnold Pellett (10) ............................... 3
Charlie Lovell (10) .............................. 3
Lana Thompson (10) .......................... 4
Harvey Brett (10) ................................ 4
Daniel Waghorne (10) ......................... 4
Ethan Marcroft (10) ............................. 5
Jordi McCracken (11) .......................... 5
Anita Davey (10) ................................. 5
Wayne Roberts (10) ............................ 6
Angel Cooper (10) ............................... 6
Natasha Standley (10) ........................ 6
Antonia Crouch (10) ............................ 7
Rhys Thompson (10) ........................... 7
Karl Crouch (10) .................................. 7
Morgan Kelly (10) ................................ 8
Aaron Marcroft (10) ............................. 8

## Arundel CE Primary School
Leon Westbrook (10) .......................... 8
Conrad May (10) ................................. 9
Finn Grimmett (7) ................................ 9
Millie Draper (7) ................................. 10
Rachel Burrows (9) ............................ 10
Leon Harris (11) ................................. 11
Michael Burrows (8) ........................... 11
Carmen Keen (7) ............................... 11
Lucy Massie (10) ............................... 12
Harrison Reid (7) ............................... 12
Lauryn Green (10) ............................. 12
Amy Hutchinson Williams (9) ............. 13

Bethany Bedford Smith (9) ................. 13
Rhian Daniel (9) ................................. 13
Juliette Gander (9) ............................. 14
Annabelle Osborne (9) ....................... 14
Felix Ramsden (9) .............................. 14
Lauren Keane (10) ............................. 15
Harry Bull (9) ...................................... 15
Alex Bayley (7) ................................... 15
Martha Baylis (9) ................................ 16
Emme Blackwell (9) ........................... 16
Samuel Cairns (10) ............................ 16
Abbie Hutchnson Williams (9) ............ 17
Jack Griffin (9) .................................... 17
Joseph Baird (9) ................................. 17
Charlotte Ward (8) ............................. 18
Victoria Wallis (9) ............................... 18
Joshua Renzulli (10) .......................... 18
Olivia Brand (7) .................................. 19

## Bishop Tufnell CE Junior School
Kathryn Mersey (9) ............................ 19
Joe Jones (10) ................................... 20
Ellen Erskine (10) .............................. 20
Lewis Cox (9) ..................................... 21
Lucy Stephenson-Gill (9) ................... 21
Liberty Clegg (11) .............................. 22
Georgia Crisp-Mills (11) ..................... 22
Maisie Mountain (10) ......................... 23
Molly Light (9) & Ferne Latham (10) ..... 23
Grace Richards (9) ............................ 24
Emily Wadey (10) ............................... 24
Josh Edwards (10) ............................. 25
Bethany Hayward (10) ....................... 25
Sophie Kingdom (10) ......................... 26
Chloe Phillips (10) .............................. 26
Olivia Tompkins (10) .......................... 27
Mitchell Cane (10) .............................. 27

| | |
|---|---|
| Owen Aldous (11) | 28 |
| James Harris (10) | 28 |
| Emily Edwards (9) | 28 |
| Amelia Simpson (9) | 29 |
| Abbeygail Longhurst (10) | 29 |
| Chloe Greene (10) | 29 |

## Blacklands Primary School

| | |
|---|---|
| Danny Power (8) | 30 |
| Chloe Johnstone (9) | 30 |
| Leon Shaw (9) | 31 |
| Adam Pearson (9) | 31 |
| Samuel Stonestreet (9) | 32 |
| Emma Gore (8) | 32 |
| Louis Tobin (9) | 32 |
| William Keeble (9) | 33 |
| Alicia Bryant (9) | 33 |
| Nathan Gain (8) | 33 |
| Stephanie Barnard (9) | 34 |
| Lewis Standivan (9) | 34 |
| Eve Steele (9) | 34 |
| Joe Buttrey (9) | 35 |
| Georgia Hall (9) | 35 |
| Isobel Law (8) | 35 |
| Harvey Mitchell-Welsh | 36 |
| Rebekah Blake (8) | 36 |
| Blade Dunford-Bleach (9) | 36 |
| Alan Crane (9) | 37 |
| Rhys Edwards (9) | 37 |
| Elliott Homewood (8) | 37 |
| Alexander Liu (8) | 38 |
| Christopher Paine (9) | 38 |

## Brede Primary School

| | |
|---|---|
| Robert Hardman (10) | 38 |
| Eliza Hannath (9) | 39 |
| Isobelle Paine (10) | 39 |
| Ellie-Jayne Adams (9) | 40 |
| Nathan Acheson (8) | 40 |
| Rebekah Bath (10) | 40 |
| Lauren Alff (8) | 41 |
| Katie Etches (10) | 41 |
| Jack Paine (9) | 41 |

| | |
|---|---|
| Charlotte Wilson (9) | 42 |
| Elizabeth Watts (7) | 42 |
| Grace Sheppard (8) | 42 |
| Abigail Pearson (9) | 43 |
| William Rollison (8) | 43 |
| Rosie Williams (9) | 43 |
| Ben Reader (7) | 44 |
| Oliver Francis (9) | 44 |
| Sarah-Louise Trundle(11) | 44 |
| James Smeed (9) | 45 |

## Dallington CE Primary School

| | |
|---|---|
| Holly Neville (11) | 45 |
| Annie Garner Hutton (10) | 46 |
| Ben Catt (10) | 46 |
| Sophie Anderson (10) | 47 |
| Sheena Moody (11) | 47 |
| Hannah Anderson (9) | 48 |
| Thomasin Quigley (10) | 48 |

## Elphinstone Community School

| | |
|---|---|
| Shannon Jeffery (9) | 48 |
| Karis Nash | 49 |
| Katriana Booth | 49 |
| Karina Golombovska | 50 |
| Olivia Ashcroft (10) | 50 |
| Lakeisha Ndlovu (10) | 51 |
| Katie May Verity (10) | 51 |
| Rhys Seetaram (11) | 52 |
| Joshua Clarie Jocham (9) | 52 |
| Charlie Barnett (11) | 53 |
| Emily Machin | 53 |
| Benjamin Newman (11) | 54 |
| Aaron James (9) | 54 |
| Nayla Mauthoor (9) | 55 |
| Jessica Wilmshurst | 55 |
| Katarina Reed | 55 |
| Troi Burnett | 56 |
| Olivia Ruff (10) | 56 |
| Kieran John | 56 |
| Kelis Kenefeck | 56 |

## Estcots Primary School

| | |
|---|---|
| Aminah Rahman (8) | 57 |
| Lauren Mansi (7) | 57 |
| Amy Gunn (9) | 58 |
| Sachin Bhangra (9) | 58 |
| Leah Harris (9) | 59 |
| Antonia Major (9) | 59 |
| Jordan Crowther (9) | 60 |
| Molly Walter (8) | 60 |
| Catalina Fernandez (8) & Jak Kettley (7) | 60 |
| Sorcha Parker Thompson (7) | 61 |
| Reid Jenden (8) | 61 |
| Kieran Taylor (8) & Erin Reakes (7) | 61 |
| Jasmine Prior (7) | 62 |
| Jade Edgar & Emelia Aylmer (7) | 62 |
| Connor Lunn (8) | 62 |
| Chloe Robinson (9) | 63 |
| Jack Gentry (7) | 63 |
| Christopher Leroy (7) | 63 |
| Danica Proctor (8) | 64 |
| Rosie Jane Sands (7) | 64 |
| Brice Major (7) | 64 |
| Mary Haines (8) & Sian Fuller (7) | 65 |
| Sophie Parsonage & Nathan Robinson (7) | 65 |
| Thomas Oomen & Melek Gunes (8) | 65 |
| Lewis Holmes (7) | 66 |
| Thomas Searle (7) | 66 |
| Dillon Stahl & Jemma Edgar (7) | 66 |
| Julia Nield (7) | 67 |
| Jayden Brown & Sam Sloan (7) | 67 |
| Ben Mooney (8) | 67 |
| Adam Stevens (7) | 67 |
| Reece Jell & Tom Wallis (7) | 68 |
| Aaron Wareing (7) & Niall Moloney (8) | 68 |
| Amy Lopez (7) | 68 |
| Matthew Tomkinson (7) | 68 |

## Ninfield CE Primary School

| | |
|---|---|
| Drew Castle (9) | 69 |
| Rebekah Hesmer (9) | 70 |
| Fallon Scott (9) | 71 |
| Charlotte Packham (9) | 72 |
| Kieran Hook (9) | 73 |
| Katie Styles (9) | 74 |
| Josie Stickells (10) | 75 |
| Molly Butler (10) | 76 |
| Nathan Creasey (9) | 77 |
| Isabelle Corby (9) | 78 |
| Daniel Abel (10) | 79 |
| Jonathan Masters (9) | 80 |
| James Kildea (9) | 81 |

## SS Peter & Paul CE Primary School, Bexhill-on-Sea

| | |
|---|---|
| Lewis Remmer (10) | 81 |
| Ayesha Shrestha (10) | 82 |
| Alexandra Lazarova (10) | 83 |
| Jade Walker (10) | 83 |
| Matthew Payne (10) | 84 |
| India Gomes (10) | 84 |
| Asia Hadleigh (10) | 85 |
| Reece Sorrell (10) | 85 |
| Lily Clough (10) | 86 |
| Amy Streets (10) | 86 |
| Katy Hannah (10) | 87 |
| Karafa-Jasmine Janneh (10) | 87 |
| Hannah Honeysett-Skippings (10) | 88 |
| Chloe Whiting (10) | 88 |
| Lucy Swatton (10) | 89 |
| Kiziah Lloyd-Graham (10) | 89 |
| Ben Chervi (10) | 90 |
| Chloe Jennings-Weir (10) | 90 |
| Hayden Fox (10) | 90 |
| Rebecca Palmer (10) | 91 |
| Ryan Blackford (10) | 91 |
| Simona Shaji (10) | 91 |
| Francesca Huff (10) | 92 |
| Connor Porthouse (10) | 92 |
| Max Giles (10) | 92 |
| Eleanor Packer (10) | 93 |
| Rowan Martyn (10) | 93 |
| Alex Skilton (10) | 93 |
| Nicola Galt (10) | 94 |
| Alex Blatchly (10) | 94 |

| | |
|---|---|
| Feaw Inplaeng (11) | 94 |
| Daniel Joseph (10) | 95 |
| Jimi Cutting (10) | 95 |
| Brandon Beal (11) | 95 |
| Jason Fox (10) | 96 |
| Joshua Bartlett (10) | 96 |
| Victoria McDonnell (10) | 96 |
| Thida Streets (11) | 97 |

## St Michael's Primary School, Withyham

| | |
|---|---|
| Leona Crawford (8) | 97 |
| Charlotte Ashby (10) | 98 |
| Molly Deer (9) | 98 |
| Wade Marais (8) | 99 |
| Kai Nelson (10) | 99 |
| Luke Morgan (8) | 100 |
| Samuel Hyde (10) | 100 |

## St Pancras Catholic Primary School, Lewes

| | |
|---|---|
| Joe Lyons (7) | 101 |
| Frankie Livesy Stephens (7) | 102 |
| Molly Osborne (10) | 102 |
| Sebastian Baynes (11) | 103 |
| Joe Windless (11) | 104 |
| Miranda Costigan (11) | 104 |
| Milton Thompson (7) | 105 |
| Morgan Harris (10) | 105 |
| Leon Reddick (7) | 106 |
| Luke Franco (10) | 106 |
| Harrison Barton (7) | 107 |
| Millie Brooks (9) | 107 |
| Teige Dillon (10) | 107 |
| Katerina Zoob (11) | 108 |
| Camille Cooper (8) | 108 |
| Henry Chown (9) | 108 |
| Beatrix Livesy Stephens (9) | 109 |
| Alfie Crowley Rata (10) | 109 |
| Joel Penrose (7) | 109 |
| Evie Flynn (7) | 110 |
| Alice Penrose (9) | 110 |
| Zofia Galloway (7) | 110 |
| Bailey Perrin (7) | 111 |

| | |
|---|---|
| Fionn Lord (11) | 111 |
| Jason Watson (9) | 111 |
| Isaac Cowler (8) | 112 |
| Phoebe Cullen (7) | 112 |
| Ellie Burall (7) | 112 |
| Jessica Smith (8) | 113 |
| Saskia Vernon (10) | 113 |

## St Philip's RC Primary School, Uckfield

| | |
|---|---|
| Matilda Taylor (10) | 113 |
| Harry Cannon (10) | 114 |
| Amy Batt (10) | 115 |
| Daisy-Anne Mayhew (10) | 116 |
| James Sutton (11) | 117 |
| Oliver Ellen (9) | 117 |
| Sean Crozier (10) | 118 |
| Isaac Gauntlett (9) | 118 |
| Bethany Lampard (10) | 119 |
| Guy Beagley (11) | 119 |
| James Rushton (10) | 120 |
| Jessica Bond (9) | 120 |
| Grace Wood (10) | 121 |
| Thomas Wasels (10) | 121 |
| Thomas Rideout (10) | 122 |
| Ciara Gaughan (10) | 122 |
| Ronan Friel (10) | 123 |
| Kathleen O'Hara (10) | 123 |
| Georgina Andrews (9) | 124 |
| Jessica Shrubbs (10) | 124 |
| Alex Burgess (10) | 125 |
| Oliver McGibbon (9) | 125 |
| Lauren Coates (10) | 126 |
| Summer Ridgley (10) | 126 |
| Phoebe Curran (10) | 127 |
| Alexandra Saunders (9) | 127 |
| Callum Smith (10) | 128 |
| Alex Azzopardi (9) | 128 |
| Ellie Brigden (9) | 129 |
| Ryan Bate (10) | 129 |
| Eve Friel (9) | 129 |
| Michael Padwick (9) | 130 |
| Nirmal Rajasekaran (9) | 130 |

| | |
|---|---|
| Thomas Wood (10) | 130 |
| Charlie Martin (11) | 131 |
| Tabitha Reed (10) | 131 |
| James Johnson (10) | 131 |
| Freddie Neill (10) | 132 |
| Jemima Beagley (9) | 132 |
| Dominic Rees (10) | 132 |
| Joseph Lower (9) | 133 |
| Beth Burchett (9) | 133 |
| William Anderson (9) | 133 |
| Thomas Lowrie (9) | 134 |
| Millie Aldred (10) | 134 |
| Shauna Page (9) | 134 |
| Adam Trueman (9) | 135 |
| James Allison (10) | 135 |

## St Robert Southwell Catholic Primary School, Horsham

| | |
|---|---|
| Niamh McGuinness (11) | 135 |
| Natasha Rogers (10) | 136 |
| Ronnie Slowinski (10) | 137 |
| Daniel Brydon (10) | 138 |
| Rachel Bowld (10) | 138 |
| Lucas Russell-Owers (9) | 139 |
| Erin Quinlivan (10) | 139 |
| Hayden Brock (9) | 140 |
| Connor Howells (10) | 140 |
| Isabelle Grant (10) | 141 |
| Daniel Longo (9) | 141 |
| Quinn D'Arcy (10) | 142 |

## Seymour Primary School

| | |
|---|---|
| Caitlin Twell (10) | 142 |
| Laiba Malik (10) | 143 |
| Charlie Knott (10) | 143 |
| Isma Saeed (10) | 144 |
| Dayna Ball (10) | 144 |
| Osman Zafar (10) | 145 |
| Jeremie Jean (10) | 145 |
| Kurt Robinson (10) | 146 |
| Georgia Edwards (10) | 146 |
| Iseoluwa Ojo (10) | 147 |
| Katie Kingshott (10) | 147 |

| | |
|---|---|
| Brinley Elliott (10) | 148 |
| Ryan Gardener (10) | 148 |
| Mark Stewart (10) | 149 |
| Liam Spiers (10) | 149 |
| Harry Philpott (10) | 150 |
| Sanjidah Uddin (10) | 150 |
| Haleema Faisal (10) | 151 |
| Akif Azeem (10) | 151 |
| Harry Brooker (11) | 152 |
| Ayesha Khan (10) | 152 |
| Javed Malik (10) | 152 |
| Kayelah Siyar (10) | 153 |

## Warninglid Primary School

| | |
|---|---|
| Stephanie Baird (10) | 153 |
| Alice Burns (10) | 153 |
| Michael Hill (10) | 154 |
| Curtis Malik (10) | 154 |
| Cameron Martin (10) | 154 |
| Harry Snell (10) | 154 |
| Ryan Fautley (11) | 155 |

## Westbourne House School

| | |
|---|---|
| Megan Baston-Steele (10) | 155 |
| Tara Noble (10) | 156 |
| Alice Jones (10) | 156 |

## West Park CE First & Middle School

| | |
|---|---|
| Joshua Payne (11) | 157 |
| Rachel Hobden (11) | 157 |
| Ossie Fish | 158 |
| Jessica Baker (11) | 158 |
| Maisie Clilverd-Buss & Leah Barnes (10) | 159 |
| Amber Hamilton (11) | 159 |
| Molly Vigor | 160 |
| Helen Skingley (11) | 160 |
| Thea Langley (10) | 160 |

## Whitehawk Primary School

| | |
|---|---|
| Katie Chadburn (11) | 161 |
| Lucy Hellier (10) | 162 |
| Danielle Harrington (10) | 163 |
| Zoe Vanhinsbergh (10) | 164 |

Lauren Stenning (11) .......................... 165
Owen Curd (11) .................................. 166
Sophie Costen (10) ........................... 167
Katana Linley (10) ............................. 168
Maisie Wheeler (10) .......................... 169
Leigh Adams (10) .............................. 170

# The Poems

*Poetry Explorers 2009 - Sussex*

## Joy Is A Yellow Sun

Joy is cheerfulness like a cold, snowy morning.
Joy is gladness like an exciting, birthday morning.
Joy is yellow like a beautiful, sunny day.
Joy is brown like a moist, chocolate cake.
Joy smells like a posy of pansies in a morning meadow.
Joy smells like a variety of fresh fruits.
Joy looks like a hot day on the beach.
Joy looks like a rainbow with all the colours.
Joy feels like the smooth texture of flowers.
Joy feels like cuddly toys that are fluffy.
Joy reminds me of my mum giving me cuddles.
Joy reminds me of my dog because he's all warm and cuddly.
Joy sounds like singing birds in the trees.
Joy sounds like gentle water in a river.

**Jamila Cope (10)**
**All Saints CE Primary School**

## Joy

Joy is the colour of yellow like the golden sun,
You might not notice but it's very fun.

Joy smells like pancakes fresh in the morning air
And when you go downstairs they will be waiting there.

Joy looks like Heaven, very happy and bright,
Be sure to bring your net to catch the golden light.

Joy feels like cotton, just woven fresh,
And when you put it on you feel refreshed.

Joy reminds me of good times with jokes,
Happiness and songs.

Joy sounds like an opera with every note perfect.

**Benjamin Bishop (11)**
**All Saints CE Primary School**

## Love And Hate

Love and hate both similar things
They make you laugh, they make you cry,
I wonder, I wonder why.

Love is the colour of fluttering pink,
And roses as red as could be.

Hate is the colour, deep dark black,
Somewhere inside you and me.

Love is happy inside you
Bouncing all around.

Hate feels all ghastly
A horrible, horrible sound.

**Jade Ennion (10)**
**All Saints CE Primary School**

## Happiness

Happiness is a beautiful bright blue,
It's floating all around.
It's loving, kind and peaceful,
And doesn't make a sound.
It smells of love and roses
It looks like a twinkling, shining star.
It feels all light and puffy
Just like I'm sure you are
It reminds me of all the good times,
The times I'm feeling blue,
It sounds like an echoing chorus
Shouting, *'I love you!'*

**Adele Wilson (11)**
**All Saints CE Primary School**

## Fun

Fun is a rainbow shining at its fullest, brightest colours.
Fun smells like a funfair with sweets and candyfloss.
Fun looks like a meadow filled with happy children laughing
And young new lovers.
Fun feels like a soft pillow filled with feathers.
Fun is like being tethered to your favourite thing
All day long.
Fun sounds like newborn birds chirping in the
Fresh morning air.

Jack Crompton (10)
**All Saints CE Primary School**

## Sadness

What a horrible day it was.
The sky was very grey, it was raining hard.
The dark, deadly cloud followed me wherever I went.

The day was sad, the day was long
I thought it would cheer me up if I sang a happy song.

So sad, so sad, I felt quite mad
I felt like giving a large roar
I just couldn't take it anymore.

Arnold Pellett (10)
**All Saints CE Primary School**

## Sadness

Sadness is a dull, gloomy and grey miserable day.
Black stale bread left to decay.
It keeps you're frown the same way round.
Your heart stops beating it's glorious sound.
A screeching echo is all you can hear.
Sadness, sadness, sadness is near.

Charlie Lovell (10)
**All Saints CE Primary School**

# Sadness

S adness is like a bunny running away forever.
A lways deep down inside the sadness of something arrives.
D eep down inside it would never leave you.
N o more happy times for me, I'm feeling glum and grey.
E very day you feel lonely.
S adness is locked in a cage and you're let out when you're happy again.
S adness and sadness and sadness is near.

**Lana Thompson (10)**
**All Saints CE Primary School**

# Excitement

Excitement is the colour orange like a newly lit fire
Shining in the darkness.
Excitement smells like a field full of lavender
Blowing in the wind.
Excitement looks like a child opening a present on his birthday.
Excitement feels like a warm blanket keeping you safe.
Excitement reminds me of all of my happy days.
Excitement sounds like a bird whistling in the trees.

**Harvey Brett (10)**
**All Saints CE Primary School**

# Happiness

Happiness shines all around you.
Happiness is the joy of love.
Happiness looks like a yellow piece of cake filled with joy.
Happiness smells like a cup of cuddles.
Happiness feels like a breezy sunny day.
Happiness is the colour of spring.
Happiness reminds you of the past of yesterday.
Happiness sounds like blue tits singing away.

**Daniel Waghorne (10)**
**All Saints CE Primary School**

## Excitement

Excitement is waking up on Christmas Day.
Excitement is a lovely Easter Day
With all the blue tits singing.
Excitement is chocolate in the afternoon.

Excitement is fireworks in the night sky.
Excitement is my heart beating with delight.
It reminds me of a chuckling child!

Ethan Marcroft (10)
**All Saints CE Primary School**

## What is Joy?

Joy is the colour green
Like a summer garden
Joy is the smell of chips
Frying in the kitchen
Joy is children smiling
Playing with their toys
Joy feels like a soft pet sleeping.

Jordi McCracken (11)
**All Saints CE Primary School**

## Happiness

Happiness is the colour of the rainbow as bright as it could be.
Happiness smells as sweet as the tender turkey on Christmas Day.
Happiness looks like blooming flowers on a summer's day.
Happiness feels like a soft tiger's coat.
Happiness reminds me of a park filled with joyful children
Playing and laughing.
Happiness sounds like the birds tweeting in the soft wind.

Anita Davey (10)
**All Saints CE Primary School**

# Sadness

Sadness is like shattered glass falling from my heart.
Sadness is the colour of happiness fading away.
Sadness is the smell of the sorrow of a thousand children.
Sadness, it looks like never seeing the sun.
Sadness, it feels like everyone tearing me apart.
Sadness reminds me of when my snake got taken away.
Sadness sounds like my skull being ripped out of my head.

**Wayne Roberts (10)**
**All Saints CE Primary School**

# Love

Love is in the air, love is a dream of princesses and queens.
Love is the colour red and a sweet kiss and hugs.
Love smells of roses and a sweet friend.
Love is happiness and love is cool.
Love makes you feel warm inside.
Love is happiness everyday, it makes you smile on a summer's day.

**Angel Cooper (10)**
**All Saints CE Primary School**

# Loss

Loss is black like a deep dark night
Loss smells like milk that has been left out
Loss looks like a scary knife
Loss feels like a bad dream
Loss reminds me of times I felt hurt
Loss sounds like crying in the night.

**Natasha Standley (10)**
**All Saints CE Primary School**

## Love

Love is the deep colour red
It's the kindest type of feeling ever read
Love is a cuddle, warm and sweet
When you have one of these you're in for a treat
Love is a heart full of truth
When you hear the greeting it means I love you.

Antonia Crouch (10)
**All Saints CE Primary School**

## Fun

Fun is like the colour yellow.
Fun is like the smell of candyfloss.
Fun looks like children in a play park.
Fun feels like a football on your trainer.
Fun reminds me of good times.
Fun sounds like an ice cream van.

Rhys Thompson (10)
**All Saints CE Primary School**

## Loss

Loss is the colour black, dark and garbage
Loss smells like a garbage truck picking up the bins
Loss looks like grey clouds floating across the sky.
Loss feels like mud and gooey.
Loss reminds me of the very muddy woods.

Karl Crouch (10)
**All Saints CE Primary School**

# Love

L ove is a lovely thing that's full of hugs and kisses.
O n a sunny day the sky is blue and the rain is gone.
V ery kind and huggable like a teddy bear, I know we'll never part.
E very day I think of you, you're always in my heart.

**Morgan Kelly (10)**
**All Saints CE Primary School**

# Loss

Loss is black and dull
It's dark and ghostly like a skull
It feels like rough stinging nettles attacking your skin
It's gruesome and lonely and doesn't let you win.

**Aaron Marcroft (10)**
**All Saints CE Primary School**

# The Lilly

Leaves scattered down from the trees and into the wavy river.
Jim sat on the dirty floor of the Lilly,
Listening to Grimy Nick snoring like a pig.

He also had Grimy Nick's dog, Snipe,
At his feet, snarling at his face.
Jim felt the boat rocking side to side
Everything was quiet for a second.

The birds stopped singing, the waves didn't rock the boat anymore.
All of a sudden a circus music started and there was loads of people doing lots of cool tricks
And then there was a boy on the side of the riverbank.
He stared at me as we went past.

**Leon Westbrook (10)**
**Arundel CE Primary School**

## A Poem About Jim's Experiences On The Lilly

It was cold and the waves were
Dancing on the Lilly,
The deep, dark blue sea was calm,
And it was so silent I could only hear
The whistling of the wind.
There was a ginormous, fierce and dangerous storm
Coming to the Lilly.
It was so fierce and dangerous
It could tear the Lilly apart.
It looked like a big patch of ink.
In the distance there was an enormous light
And it was as red as fire.
The black haunted ship rocked
Like a storm was attacking it.
And then there was only the sea
That looked like black ink.

Conrad May (10)
**Arundel CE Primary School**

## The Grasshopper

The grasshopper hopped happily all day.
Over the tallest grass you could imagine.
He was so happy that he missed the horrible dark hole
So he fell down it.
It was full of humongous brown walls.
But then he saw a speck of light.
He made a big jump out of the hole but then he saw a
humongous mole
The grasshopper was small and green
And he had bendy legs
But the mole was big and brown
And he had small and strong legs.

Finn Grimmett (7)
**Arundel CE Primary School**

# Escape

I am cold
I am terrified
I am lost
I sleep in boxes
I am scared
I want to go home
It's horrible out here
But I am free
I have nothing to eat and drink
I am heartbroken
But I have freedom.

**Millie Draper (7)**
**Arundel CE Primary School**

# Exhaustion

Exhaustion is black,
Like a witch's cat,
It tastes like old crumbs,
The food for a rat.
It smells like mud,
Slushy and thick.
It looks like a person.
Sweaty and sick.
It sounds like a great and heavy sigh,
It feels like not sleeping until it's night.

**Rachel Burrows (9)**
**Arundel CE Primary School**

## The Lilly

It was so silent that Jim could hear
The waves speaking to the Lilly.

It was so still Jim could see the
Street buildings calmly swapping place.

It was so hushed Jim could hear the
Sky dancing.

It was so hushed, still and silent
That Jim could hear everything and could see the world waking up.

Leon Harris (11)
**Arundel CE Primary School**

## Escape

I am slinky like a cat
But I am terrified
I have nowhere to go
I hate life outside
I'm hidden in the dark
All I can hear is people laughing
And the carts bumping by
The main thing is that I'm free!

Michael Burrows (8)
**Arundel CE Primary School**

## Bear

The cuddly bear has brown hair.
He has a small nose.
The cuddly bear has big eyes.
The cuddly bear has a smiley face.
The bear is fun.
They are cute.
They are lazy until they need to eat.

Carmen Keen (7)
**Arundel CE Primary School**

# The Lilly

It was so calm you could hear the wind
Eating away the distant voices of the circus people!
It was so quiet that you could hear the sludge
Wiping itself against the battered boat!
Moving through the midnight sky,
The stars shone above the town.
It was so still that you could feel your thoughts
Whooshing through your shivering head!

**Lucy Massie (10)**
**Arundel CE Primary School**

# The Python

The python slithers slow and silent
Past a stack of straw.
He smells the air with his tongue
And smells danger.
So he slithers away quickly.
He slithers past a mouse and
Attacked it and ate it.
Then slithered back to its den.

**Harrison Reid (7)**
**Arundel CE Primary School**

# The Wind

Hear the wind rustle on the leaves in the autumn,
See them fall down outside your window,
Smell the fresh air,
It smells so fine,
Hear the message that God is telling you.

Listen to the things He tells you.
Then listen to the rain patter down on your rooftop in the winter!

**Lauryn Green (10)**
**Arundel CE Primary School**

## Embarrassed

Embarrassed is the colour of a red shiny apple.
It tastes like toast and jam for breakfast.
It smells like red hot fire in your eyes.
It looks like disgusting mouldy bread with red cream.
It sounds like someone is getting scared or chased
In the cold wavy sea.
It feels like hard cheeks with a Yorkshire pudding.

**Amy Hutchinson Williams (9)**
**Arundel CE Primary School**

## Fear!

Fear is black like a witch's hat.
Fear is like a gentle touch
Of a snake's bite.
Fear looks like a rumble of thunder
Fear feels like a ghost nearby.
Fear sounds like a tornado.
It feels like mud in my face.

**Bethany Bedford Smith (9)**
**Arundel CE Primary School**

## Unsettled

Unsettled is the colour of autumn leaves,
It tastes like old blue cheese,
It smells like a distant fire,
And looks like rusting wire,
It sounds like cracking whips,
And feels like broken sticks,
Unsettled is someone near you.

**Rhian Daniel (9)**
**Arundel CE Primary School**

## Fear

Fear is covered with terrifying bugs.
It feels like a wet damp area
That feels like it's closing upon you.
It smells like a sausage.
It looks like a grey, black place.
It sounds like a fire closing upon you.
It feels like the end of you.

**Juliette Gander (9)**
**Arundel CE Primary School**

## Sadness

Sadness is grey like a gloomy rain cloud.
Sadness tastes sour and like rotten eggs
Sadness smells damp, dirty and smoky.
Sadness looks dark lonely and shy.
Sadness sounds like screams of pain.
Sadness feels slimy, gooey and hard.
Sadness is always near you.

**Annabelle Osborne (9)**
**Arundel CE Primary School**

## Fear

Its colour is dark black
It tastes like burnt toast
It smells like mouldy cheese spread
It looks like a hand print on a table
It sounds like screams of zombies
It feels like a rusty goalpost
Fear is all around you like a ghost.

**Felix Ramsden (9)**
**Arundel CE Primary School**

## Love!

Love is the colour of a rose, red and round,
It tastes like chocolates,
It smells like a sunflower,
It looks pretty in pink with the sun,
It feels soft and cuddly and never any frowns around!
It sounds like the first kiss of life!

**Lauren Keane (10)**
**Arundel CE Primary School**

## Anger

Anger is red like evil.
It tastes like red hot chillies.
It smells like burning wood.
It looks like fire bursting out of the ground.
It sounds like someone laughing evilly.
It feels like fire burning you.

**Harry Bull (9)**
**Arundel CE Primary School**

## The Stag

Rushing through the corn
The white stag standing as still as a tree.
So he was calm eating corn
Until a tiger rushed out and scared him.
The stag rushed to hide.
The beautiful white stag could not be seen.

**Alex Bayley (7)**
**Arundel CE Primary School**

# Fear

Fear is black like someone has turned the lights out on your life.
Fear tastes like old rice pudding and lumpy gravy.
Fear smells like a musty loft.
Fear looks like time passing through an eye.
Fear sounds like an evil cackle.
Fear feels like a bony hand tiptoeing down your spine.

**Martha Baylis (9)**
**Arundel CE Primary School**

# Angry

It is like red blood.
It tastes like mouldy cabbage.
It smells like sweaty people.
It looks like you are going to blow up.
It sounds spooky.
It feels like rotten goo.

**Emme Blackwell (9)**
**Arundel CE Primary School**

# Eager

Eager is the colour yellow
Eager tastes like chocolate mud pie
Eager smells like rose, red roses
Eager looks like the yellow of lightning
Eager sounds like a dog panting
Eager feels like you're ready to go.

**Samuel Cairns (10)**
**Arundel CE Primary School**

## Scared

Scared is green
It tastes like a mouldy banana
It smells like smoke
It looks like lumpy custard
It sounds like thunder
It feels like slime.

**Abbie Hutchnson Williams (9)**
**Arundel CE Primary School**

## Upset

Upset is grey
It tastes like old beetroot
Upset smells like wet mud
It looks like grey clouds
Upset sounds like a lion roaring in your ear
It feels like a mouldy banana.

**Jack Griffin (9)**
**Arundel CE Primary School**

## Joy

Joy is blue as the sky.
Joy tastes like apple and blackberry crumble.
Joy smells like a toffee apple.
Joy looks like a blue bouncy ball.
Joy is like a bird singing a tune.
Joy feels like a light wind in the air.

**Joseph Baird (9)**
**Arundel CE Primary School**

## The Bird

The brown feathery bird flew through the hot air
And did a high-pitched squawk.
His sharp claws landed with his tasty prey.
He took his tea home and ate it with his family.
The family then went to fly together.

**Charlotte Ward (8)**
**Arundel CE Primary School**

## Happy

It tastes like melted chocolate.
It smells like fresh air.
It looks like the sunset.
It sounds like laughter.
It feels like the warmth of my mother's hand.

**Victoria Wallis (9)**
**Arundel CE Primary School**

## Anger

Anger is bright red.
It tastes like fresh flesh.
Anger smells like fresh blood.
It sounds like a loud scream.
It feels like punching a hole in the wall.

**Joshua Renzulli (10)**
**Arundel CE Primary School**

## The Butterfly

The elegant butterfly flew through the tall wavy trees.
She glided onto a branch.
She had beautiful colourful wings
She flies down from the sky.

Olivia Brand (7)
**Arundel CE Primary School**

## The Poem

What shall I write,
Where shall I go?
How will it happen?
I don't know.
What will the start be?
How will it end?
Write about enemies,
Write about friends.
Will it need rhyming?
Should it be funny?
Will it be raining
Or should it be sunny?

I have no ideas,
My mind is blank,
The ticking clock
Like a marching tank,
This is such a challenge,
Just my luck,
Oh good heavens,
I'm completely stuck.
Poems are tricky,
I can't get it done,
Hang on a second
I've just written one!

Kathryn Mersey (9)
**Bishop Tufnell CE Junior School**

# Chocolate

Chocolate, oh chocolate
So many different types
Galaxy, Mars and Milky way
If I eat one of them, *Mmmm*!
It will definitely make my day
Chocolate, oh chocolate
So many different flavours
Orange, mint and white
Once I have one of them
*Mmmm*! I feel alright
Chocolate, oh chocolate
So many different sizes
Medium. Big and small
If I scoff one of them
*Mmmm*, I won't feel bad at all
Chocolate, oh chocolate
So many different fillings
Caramel, soft and chunky
If I eat one of them
*Mmmm* I will have enough energy to be funky.

**Joe Jones (10)**
**Bishop Tufnell CE Junior School**

# Time

Time goes fast.
Time goes slow.
Time is long.
Time is short.
Time is analogue.
Time is digital.
Time is counting.
For however long.
Up to sixty or maybe more
But the time is half-past two!

**Ellen Erskine (10)**
**Bishop Tufnell CE Junior School**

## Waddle

Waddle, waddle all around.
Waddle, waddle, safe and sound.
Chat, chat with your friends.
Chat, chat to your pet.
Shush, shush in the theatre,
Shush in the book room.
Fight, fight at the dojo.
Surf, surf at the cove.
Secret agents everywhere.
Secret agents over there.
From the beacon I can see
Stranded penguins waving at me.
In the nightclub what might that be?
A secret doorway maybe.
Be real cool.
Take a visit to the pool.
Support a team, blue or green.
Waddle, waddle all around.

**Lewis Cox (9)**
**Bishop Tufnell CE Junior School**

## Dreaming

This is my dream, anything could happen.
I could be star.
I could be a super-model,
Or maybe I could work with penguins.
*Waddle, waddle, waddle!*
I could choose what to do and who to be and maybe,
I could fly an aeroplane and only just me!
I would like to be a runner, running in a race.
And I hope one day to see that look upon your face!
I dream while I am sleeping,
I dream while I'm awake, but every time I dream,
I dream about a flowing lake.

**Lucy Stephenson-Gill (9)**
**Bishop Tufnell CE Junior School**

# Seasons

Spring is bouncy, with a new start,
Fresh flowers, green lawns, a joy to my heart.
Hear the birds singing, the church bells ringing,
Spring is a joy to my heart.
Summer is warm, a time for the beach,
If your dad gets burnt prepare for a screech,
Warm sea waves for everyone,
Come and join in with the fun.
Autumn is crisp, with Hallowe'en goods,
Red, yellow and orange fills the woods,
It's getting colder and colder, the winds started humming:
I'm pretty sure winter's coming.
Winter is here, get ready for snow,
So warm up by the fire with hot cocoa,
Christmas is coming, with presents to spare,
Happy children everywhere!
That's the seasons from all year round,
From high in the sky to low on the ground.

**Liberty Clegg (11)**
**Bishop Tufnell CE Junior School**

# Fatal

I woke up early that morning and I struggled to breathe,
My heart beating, I ran out the front door
And I knew I was never going to go back.
I ran and ran until I had to stop.
I couldn't believe I did it,
I got a flashback of the dead body and all the blood on my fingers.
But something wasn't right, I fell,
I found myself in a wood.
My sight went blurry.
I saw darkness.
I laid there and never woke up.

**Georgia Crisp-Mills (11)**
**Bishop Tufnell CE Junior School**

## My Dream World

My dream world is totally magic,
It can be fun or also tragic,
I look around and all I see,
A big world surrounding me!

I jump to each lily pad,
Coming up with more ideas,
I say, 'No time for tears!'

My head is overflowing,
Everything is glowing,
Every idea pops out,
'Yay!' I shout!

My dream world is the best,
No time for rest!
But I close my eyes,
And slowly fall asleep.

Maisie Mountain (10)
**Bishop Tufnell CE Junior School**

## My Pencil Case Is A Time Travelling Machine!

My pencil case is a time travelling machine,
It helps me with my classes,
Although sometimes I leave behind my glasses,
Which help me see.
So I type in the wrong numbers on my calculator,
And zoom to 1973!
I typed this,
And I typed that,
I even have to stop at the services,
To get some sweets,
Then I zoom off,
Listening to the latest beats 'yo!

Molly Light (9) & Ferne Latham (10)
**Bishop Tufnell CE Junior School**

# Memories

Memories are fun,
Exciting and amazing,
Things to look back on,
And putting a smile on your face,
Memories are useful,
They can be happy and sad,
And emotional too,
How happy can they be?
It's up to you!

Memories are fun,
When times are amazing you can write them down,
And remember them whenever,
You make memories happen,
And fate doesn't decide everything.

**Grace Richards (9)**
**Bishop Tufnell CE Junior School**

# My World

My world is a fairy tale,
A book of spells,
A never-ending dream,
A slide to fortune,
And fame on the side,
Including dinner with the Queen,
I could fly on a magic carpet,
I could look over the sea,
I could run a race and even win,
I could be a princess,
Or anything I want to be,
I'm not a number 2 or 3,
It's my world I'm
*Me!*

**Emily Wadey (10)**
**Bishop Tufnell CE Junior School**

## Sweets

Sweets, oh! Sweets, such wonderful treats
There are gobstoppers, marshmallows
As far as the eye can see.
Sweets, oh! Sweets, such wonderful treats
There are mints, there are chewies
All around the shop.
Sweets, oh! Sweets, such wonderful treats
There are long ones and short ones
So many different sizes.
Sweets, oh! Sweets, such wonderful treats
There are pink ones and green ones and blue and lots more.
Sweets, oh! Sweets, such wonderful treats
There are sticky ones and ones that squirt
They are so tasty!

Josh Edwards (10)
**Bishop Tufnell CE Junior School**

## Autumn

Autumn is yellow,
Autumn is red,
I think of autumn when I'm in bed.

Shimmering streams,
Shining sunbeams,
Don't forget Hallowe'en.

Pumpkin faces,
In different places,
Spooky ghosts and witches.

It's getting colder and colder,
The wind is humming,
I'm pretty sure winter's coming.

Bethany Hayward (10)
**Bishop Tufnell CE Junior School**

## Space

My greatest wish is to go into space, and see what I can find.
My dad says a lot of rubbish but I bet bacon rind.
I have to see the aliens plus the solar system
And to see if any weird monsters have risen.

There might be satellite dishes, there might be rockets in flight,
All of the planets will be at great height.
Plus supernovas ready to explode,
Fizzling shooting stars packed with overload.

Silvery shooting comets flying here and there,
Millions of twinkling stars which look like golden hair,
Everything is so amazing, I'll tell you one more time. . .
*My greatest wish is to go into space!*

**Sophie Kingdom (10)**
**Bishop Tufnell CE Junior School**

## Breakfast Time

*'Mmmmmmm!'* I can smell bacon,
I can smell toast.
I can smell sausage,
It could be a roast!

The smell is getting closer
*'Ooooooo!'* it smells so good.
It's creeping across the landing,
That is some great food.

It's coming in my bedroom,
It's going near my bed.
It's landed on my lap,
And now I have been fed.

**Chloe Phillips (10)**
**Bishop Tufnell CE Junior School**

## My Life

My life is a dream,
Anything can happen,
I can wish upon a star,
Or fly into space,
I can be who I want to be,
Whenever I want,
I can fly into my dreams,
And never come out,
I can be myself,
All the time
I'm *me!*

Olivia Tompkins (10)
**Bishop Tufnell CE Junior School**

## My Pet Copper

I love Copper, he's my pet,
He can get very wet,
Copper loves to dress up,
And drink tea from a cup,
This is my pet Copper.

Copper loves to sleep on my bed,
He is treated well and is always fed,
Copper needs a bath,
And when he howls it makes me laugh,
This is my pet Copper.

Mitchell Cane (10)
**Bishop Tufnell CE Junior School**

# Once There Was A. . .

Once there was a crocodile as long as could be,
Once there was a dinosaur running free.

Once there was a really cool monkey,
Once there was a tiger, it was really funky.

Once there was a giraffe as high as the sky,
Once there was a spider that loved pie.

Once there was a butterfly, flying with glee,
Once there was a snake as cool as could be.

**Owen Aldous (11)**
**Bishop Tufnell CE Junior School**

# My Little Sister

I have a little sister, she is funny and nice
She is always running and jumping around
Then again she is always falling down
When I fall over she laughs and laughs

We sometimes play hide-and-seek
On her turn to seek she always peeps
Sometimes she hides under my bed but giggles and giggles
So I go over and say '*Boo!*'

**James Harris (10)**
**Bishop Tufnell CE Junior School**

# Happy Me

I am happy, I am sad.
I am happy, I am glad.
I am happy and so are you.
Come on now let's get happy.
I am happy, leave me be,
I am happy me!

**Emily Edwards (9)**
**Bishop Tufnell CE Junior School**

## Strange World

Imagine having the sky in your pie,
Imagine having caterpillars in your sandwich,
Imagine being able to eat the moon and drink the stars,
Imagine being able to live for as long as you want,
Imagine having guitars in the bath,
Imagine your brothers falling for all your jokes,
Now that would be fun.
What a weird world it would be!

**Amelia Simpson (9)**
**Bishop Tufnell CE Junior School**

## Books

I read in the day, I read at night,
My books are never out of sight.
Big books, small books, any book will do,
My books are never out of sight.
I read inside, I read outside,
My books are never out of sight.
But one day I looked for my book but I couldn't find it,
Oh no, my books are out of sight, what a fright!

**Abbeygail Longhurst (10)**
**Bishop Tufnell CE Junior School**

## My Life

My life is good and bad
It is family and friends *but*
I still love them and they love me
I love the time to spend with my mum and stepdad
I love them more than ever, they give good cuddles.

**Chloe Greene (10)**
**Bishop Tufnell CE Junior School**

## A Recipe For A Perfect Goal

Take a talented boy
Mix in a sweaty leather ball
And 2 goals
Stir for 4 minutes
Add some grass and a goalie's shoes and shin pads for 22
Take a centre and the offside rule
Two teams plus coloured T-shirts
Plus one referee
Let it boil for 45 minutes
Take a break
Heat again for 45 minutes
Look at the results!

**Danny Power (8)**
**Blacklands Primary School**

## A Recipe For A Rainbow

Ingredients:
Paint, glue, love, sun and rain and lots more.
Get some hair from the finest lady.
Boil some paint in the oven and slap it on.
Pour some glue into the sky.
Add some love from the happiest cat.
Guide the sun to your rainbow.
Fry some rain until it shines.
Fold some people into a box.
Mash broken hearts and mould them again.
Knead love into mud and throw it into the air.
And there's your rainbow.

**Chloe Johnstone (9)**
**Blacklands Primary School**

## Sounds Of Silence

Can you hear the steps of a ladybird
Or the grass growing in your garden?
Have you heard the pages of a book turn
Or shavings falling into a bin?
Can you hear your teeth growing
Or a bee taking pollen from a flower?
Have you heard your hair growing
Or a butterfly's wings fluttering?
Can you hear a fish's heart beating
Or its tail swishing through the water?

**Leon Shaw (9)**
**Blacklands Primary School**

## A Recipe For A Good Friend

Take one innocent kid
Add a smile
Pour in some fall outs
Fry them playing in the sun
Boil them in truthful oil till they go brown
Grate some funny
Sprinkle the pieces of funny in
Mix in some kind
Cut into a human shape again
And it's done.

**Adam Pearson (9)**
**Blacklands Primary School**

# A Recipe For An Evil Gerbil!

You take the Devil's brain out
Then you steal hair from the hairdressers
Then shave the feet and shave the ears
Get a Smart car engine
Add the suspension and put an accelerator in the gerbil
And put the gearbox in
Then charge him up on a charger
Liam will give it the kiss of life
That's how you make an evil gerbil.

**Samuel Stonestreet (9)**
**Blacklands Primary School**

# A Recipe For A Poem

Take a rhyming genius
Add a clever brain
Drizzle some poetry books
In a different bowl that looks the same
Then bake it together
Pour the books in
Take it out of the oven
Decorate with words
Then eat it and you will rhyme like mad!

**Emma Gore (8)**
**Blacklands Primary School**

# Sounds Of Silence

Can you hear a cake cooking?
Have you heard the sound of a digital clock?
Can you here the board being rubbed or a basketball being thrown?
Have you heard the butterfly slapping its wings?
Can you hear a cat eating its food?
Have you heard a dog wagging its tail?

**Louis Tobin (9)**
**Blacklands Primary School**

*Poetry Explorers 2009 - Sussex*

## A Recipe For A Perfect Skateboard!

Take some super mini jets, two pairs of wheels
And a super grippy board of wood,
And a lifetime supply of food and drink and last a gold auto button.

Steal two super mini jets from a stunt trolley,
Next attach the auto button and the wheels for fun,
Also add the jets on the sides.

Now somehow mix the food and drink in the skateboard
And put a whole load of fun in it!

William Keeble (9)
**Blacklands Primary School**

## The Sound Of Silence

Have you heard an empty chair waiting to be sat on?
Can you hear the footsteps of an ant?
Have you heard sharpenings fall on the floor?
Can you hear a butterfly's wing beat in the air?
Have you heard a fish's tail swishing in the water?
Can you hear the wingbeat of a bird in the sky?
Have you heard the sound of a spider spinning its web?
Can you hear the footsteps of a ladybird patting along the floor?

Alicia Bryant (9)
**Blacklands Primary School**

## Recipe For A Monster

Take one scary head
Add a fat, smelly body
Mix in 5 sharp daggers and put them as teeth
Put some blood on the ends
Pour in some snot and mix with goo
With rotten food all over the body

You have a monster!

Nathan Gain (8)
**Blacklands Primary School**

# The Sound Of Silence

Have you heard the sun shining on a summer's day?
Have you heard a feather falling on a dusty floor?
Can you hear a spider on its web waiting for its dinner?
Can you hear a cake baking in the oven?
Have you heard a butterfly flying over the flowers in the garden?
Have you heard the mouse sleeping in its cage?
Can you hear the dark streets at midnight?
Can you hear the leaves falling off the tree?

**Stephanie Barnard (9)**
**Blacklands Primary School**

# Sounds Of Silence

Can you hear the clouds moving or the sun shining?
Can you hear the book being read?
Have you heard the trees or the wind blowing?
Can you hear the pages of a book being turned?
Can you hear a leaf hitting the ground?
Can you hear your teeth growing?
Can you hear an old man's beard moving in the wind?
Can you hear the bushes growing in the garden?

**Lewis Standivan (9)**
**Blacklands Primary School**

# A Recipe For A Good Friend

Take one cube of sugar
Then mix it with grain
Add some sweet candy
Then do it again
Add a human head
Then say goodnight
Take a good bite. . .
Of chocolate.

**Eve Steele (9)**
**Blacklands Primary School**

## A Recipe For A Good Football Team

Get 11 or more people and the best football trainer in the world,
Then get a good manager and an excellent coach
And mix it all together.
Pour in a blue and white stadium,
Boil it all.
Pour it onto a great big field.
Train your people,
Then organise a match with a winning team and you should win!

Joe Buttrey (9)
**Blacklands Primary School**

## A Recipe For A Lizard

Take the points from the top of an ancient Egyptian pyramid,
Some slimy goo, and some sharp claws,
Get the brain of a human and give it a spring to jump really high.
Cut the brain out of a human's head and select the good bits.
Slice the points from the tops of the ancient Egyptian pyramids.
Blend some slimy goo and some sharp claws,
Chop a spring in half and add it to the sharp claws.
Roast for 10 years then you have a cool lizard.

Georgia Hall (9)
**Blacklands Primary School**

## A Recipe For Hallowe'en

Take a black, pointed hat
Take a dark, long cloak
Take a silly, fat cat
Take some pointed shoes
Take a big, thin broom
Finally pick up a cauldron
And then you've made a Hallowe'en costume.

Isobel Law (8)
**Blacklands Primary School**

## A Recipe For A Disaster

Take one spicy, hot meatball,
Pour on an angry lobster,
Fry one evil devil,
Stir in one rotten egg,
Bake for 2 mins,
Decorate it with dragons' claws
And you should have my sister.

**Harvey Mitchell-Welsh**
**Blacklands Primary School**

## A Recipe For A Scare

Take a hairy, scary monster
And a bowl of ghosts
Take some butter and jam
Then a slice of toast
Get some snowy white fangs
And some pointy, sharp claws
Then maybe some huge dino roars!

**Rebekah Blake (8)**
**Blacklands Primary School**

## Sounds Of Silence

Can you hear an eagle gliding next to the shimmering sun?
Can you hear a ladybird fluttering in the sky?
Can you hear a rubber band springing in mid-air?
Can you hear a horse snore or a granny coming for a visit?
Have you heard Blade get bored or a sphinx smash?
Can you hear wheat growing or a glow worm glowing?

**Blade Dunford-Bleach (9)**
**Blacklands Primary School**

## A Recipe For A Happy Christmas

Take one 25th of December
Mix in some presents, family and laughter
Add in turkey and chocolate
Pour in some amazing TV
Decorate one fireplace with tinsel and bells
Roast for 24 hours.

Alan Crane (9)
**Blacklands Primary School**

## Recipe For A Happy Baby

Take one bundle of joy
Mix in some nappies and baby wipes
Add some milk
Play with baby for a long time
Tickle them and say, 'Peek-a-boo!'
You will end up with one happy baby!

Rhys Edwards (9)
**Blacklands Primary School**

## A Recipe For A Lovely Mum

Take one lovely lady
Mix in 2 naughty children
Add a sweet sister
Pour in some washing up
And some ironing
Add a lovely heart too!

Elliott Homewood (8)
**Blacklands Primary School**

## Recipe For A Dream

Take one comfy bed, a bedtime story
Make sure it is not scary
And a little child, a goodnight hug
Stir together until he falls asleep
And this will make a dream.

**Alexander Liu (8)**
**Blacklands Primary School**

## A Recipe For A Sun

Take a bundle of light as bright as a star,
Add some love and care,
Mix a pile of sweetness,
Boil the ingredients with a pinch of God
And serve them up to the people of the world!

**Christopher Paine (9)**
**Blacklands Primary School**

## Pain

Pain is as red as blood
And as dark as the night sky.

Pain smells like a thousand teardrops
From a hundred people.

Pain sounds like two hundred ghosts
Screaming in the gloom-filled sky.

Pain is a man staring you in the face
Dragging you into the darkness. . .

**Robert Hardman (10)**
**Brede Primary School**

## Fun

Fun smells of a chocolate ice cream with multicoloured sprinkles.
Fun is the colours red, blue, yellow and green
And spreads everywhere around you.
It pulls you along to have fun.
Red is for love and happiness,
Blue is for bouncing around,
Yellow is the bright sun for a nice sunny picnic day
And green is for a very happy, smiley face.
Fun sounds like a birthday being celebrated
With balloons hovering in the air next door.
Fun tastes of a chocolate cake being decorated and waiting to be eaten.
Fun looks like children bouncing around, being joyful.
Fun feels like you're having butterflies in your stomach because you're excited.
Fun reminds me of a happy holiday that I've had with my
best friends.

**Eliza Hannath (9)**
**Brede Primary School**

## Love

Love is a red rose blossoming in my heart.
Love smells of my mum's homemade chocolate cake
Made with tenderness.
Love is the sound of a cat purring in the blazing sun.
Love is warm and comforting like a soft blanket
Wrapped around my cold shoulders.
Love tastes of Galaxy chocolate in front of the TV.
Love is a glorious sunset in my heart.
Love reminds me of the love that the mother has for her child.

**Isobelle Paine (10)**
**Brede Primary School**

## Fun, Fun, Fun

Fun is like a rainbow in the sky all the time
Fun is like having a shiver down my spine of happiness
Fun is not something everyone has
Fun is what we all deserve
So no one will take it away from me and you
Fun is something that feels like it will never end
So come on and celebrate with me
And bring your friends along
So we all can have fun!

**Ellie-Jayne Adams (9)**
**Brede Primary School**

## Fun

Fun sounds like screaming children running around in the park.
Fun is the yellow of the sun on a hot day,
As little children play in the sea.
Fun is the scent of ice cream as little boys run to the
Ice cream truck.
Fun looks like happy children playing.
Fun tastes like cold water you've just drunk after running about.
Fun reminds me of the first friend I ever had.
Fun feels like damp grass on the ground after it's been raining.

**Nathan Acheson (8)**
**Brede Primary School**

## Happiness

Happiness is where you can let your feelings burst out in the air,
Like a pink balloon popping.
Happiness is a big smiley face on the world.
Happiness is tingly feelings inside of me that go away.
Happiness tastes of a milk-coloured birthday cake.
Happiness smells of a basket of flowers.

**Rebekah Bath (10)**
**Brede Primary School**

## Anger

Anger is red with rage, like when a child steals
her brother's money.
Anger sounds like a mother screaming at her child.
Anger looks like a horrid, bright red colour.
Anger reminds me of a dad sending a child to bed.
Anger smells of smelly, shouting breath.
Anger has a horrid sour taste.
Anger is a horrible feeling like you want to scream your head off.

**Lauren Alff (8)**
**Brede Primary School**

## Surprise

Surprise is a dashing bright yellow,
Jumping at you like a tiger.
Surprise is the commotion of a balloon popping in your ear.
Surprise is the flavour of a bitter strawberry,
That leaves a shocking taste that you weren't expecting.
Surprise is all your favourite dreams coming true.
Surprise looks like everything you ever wanted.
Surprise reminds me of a firework going up into the sky rapidly.

**Katie Etches (10)**
**Brede Primary School**

## Pain Is Bad

Pain is a punch in the back really hard
Pain sounds as if there is a bone cracking in your body
Pain is dark grey as if the world has turned evil
Pain looks as if you're in a haunted house in your heart
Pain reminds me of falling out of bed
Pain tastes like dust from the sky
Pain smells like a rotten apple in a rotten garden.

**Jack Paine (9)**
**Brede Primary School**

## Sadness

Sadness smells of salty water in the sea.
Sadness tastes of a sour lemon.
The black sadness feels like your heart is being dragged out.
Sadness sounds like I'm all alone
And no one is there for me.
Sadness is a heart that is broken in half.
Sadness reminds me of someone dying.

**Charlotte Wilson (9)**
**Brede Primary School**

## Courage

Courage looks like someone standing up for someone else.
Courage is as white as snow.
Courage reminds me of my brother.
Courage sounds like someone arguing, thinking they are going to win.
Courage feels like someone fighting.
Courage tastes like victory when you win something.

**Elizabeth Watts (7)**
**Brede Primary School**

## Silence

Silence is so quiet it's almost impossible for you to speak.
Silence sounds like the whispering of a child.
Silence smells of little children being quiet.
Silence reminds me of the day I could not speak.
Silence is the colour of the blossom on the beautiful trees.
Silence feels so surprising, every child likes it.
Silence tastes like quiet sweet people.

**Grace Sheppard (8)**
**Brede Primary School**

## Fear

Fear is a dark black night.
Fear smells of old dusty cobwebs.
Fear sounds of scraping claws on the window pane.
Fear tastes like the desert sand drying up my mouth.
Fear is loads of monsters coming towards me.
Fear feels like a devil inside my heart.
Fear reminds me of darts shooting me from above.

**Abigail Pearson (9)**
**Brede Primary School**

## Wonder

Wonder is the colour orange, like autumn leaves
Wonder feels like my rugby team wining the cup.
Wonder looks like someone putting their finger on their chin.
Wonder is worrying, 'Are we going to catch the aeroplane?'
Wonder sounds like someone humming to themselves.
Wonder tastes like passanda coconut curry washing over my tongue.
Wonder is the smell of red roses in springtime.

**William Rollison (8)**
**Brede Primary School**

## Fun

Fun is a bright, colourful rainbow.
Fun feels like a fast roller coaster ride with my friend.
Fun reminds me of playing with my friends.
Fun tastes of a yummy banana split with sprinkles.
Fun smells of tasty sweets on my birthday.
Fun sounds like loud music at a disco.
Fun is a big lollipop at the funfair.

**Rosie Williams (9)**
**Brede Primary School**

# Wonder

Wonder reminds me of a child's face after opening a present.
Wonder smells of a hot chocolate on a cold day.
Wonder sounds like my friend asking to play with me.
Wonder is blue, green and sometimes yellow like a rainbow.
Wonder looks like my friend winning a race.
Wonder feels like going to France on a ferry.
Wonder tastes like chocolate.

**Ben Reader (7)**
**Brede Primary School**

# Pain Hurts

Pain is black, as black as a night in winter
Pain has a stench of fresh blood from a wound
Pain sounds like someone crying for help
Pain looks like the place you are in will never end
Pain tastes as if your mouth is bleeding
Pain feels like never-ending agony
Pain reminds me of the time I fell out of my bunk bed.

**Oliver Francis (9)**
**Brede Primary School**

# Sadness

Sadness reminds me of leaving my mummy.
Sadness is a black crow pecking my heart out.
Sadness smells of salty water from the ocean wide.
Sadness is a swarm of evil black crows tearing my heart apart.
Sadness tastes like peppery water.
Sadness is the weeping of a newborn baby.

**Sarah-Louise Trundle(11)**
**Brede Primary School**

## Sir Francis Drake

Drake sailed, around he went.
He sailed and sailed.
He never stopped.
Then he caught sight of the Pacific Ocean.
He was very pleased.
But then he died at sea.

**James Smeed (9)**
**Brede Primary School**

## The Sea

The sea is a bouncing kangaroo,
Proud and loud.
She bounces on the beach all day.
With her foamy feet appearing then
Disappearing when she jumps in the air.
Then the kangaroo grabs some stones to nibble for later.

She goes back and forth
On summer nights.
While people skim the stones,
The kangaroo flings them across.
She springs up in the night crashing
Against the rocks.

In the winter she curls up in a cave
And snores.
When boats wake her,
She tosses them in the air.
But on calm winter days,
With snowdrops in the gardens,
She just rolls and lets people throw stony food for her to gobble up
During the cold nights.

**Holly Neville (11)**
**Dallington CE Primary School**

# The Sea

The sea is a galloping horse,
Beautiful and proud,
She canters upon the beach,
With pounding hooves.
Then she disappears away again,
Her silky mane flies out,
And her swishing tail makes a calming noise.

When she is angry she kicks out at the cliffs,
Making rocks fall,
She makes ships sink with her angry gallop,
She leaps into the air on her slender legs,
And takes people from the beach,
Never to be seen again.

But when summer comes,
She is calm and sweet
And frolics with the children in the sand,
She trots on her dainty legs,
And brings back shells for sandcastles.
Then she lies down for a rest and lets people play on her back.

Annie Garner Hutton (10)
**Dallington CE Primary School**

# The Sea

The sea is like a tree frog, croaking all day long,
Hopping up the cliff,
Bouncing on the shore taking in anything it can find.

In the summer days he settles down and goes with
The soft summer breeze.
When people come along and wake him from his
Slumber he leaps at them and gets them wet.

In the winter days, he settles down and goes to sleep.
When those trawlers come he gets rough.

Ben Catt (10)
**Dallington CE Primary School**

## The Sea

The sea is a young stallion,
As white as a sparkling pearl.
He gallops along the beaches all day,
With his clashing hooves and
Flowing mane.

When winter comes,
He will become Hell's Dark Angel,
Leaping over rotting rocks and rearing at the
Laughing sun.

But when the sun begins to shine
And the weather is fine,
He gives his riders on saddles
The time of their life.

**Sophie Anderson (10)**
**Dallington CE Primary School**

## The Sea

The sea is a charging elephant
Large and loud
She crashes on to the beach
Further and further she goes up
After hours she pulls back
The splishing and splashing water
Spurting trunk, drenching everything it reaches
The great 'Ele' groans
Stomping her feet and making the rocks rumble

When the still day turns to a stormy night
And the moon's shudder is in the wind
She roams around turning into the wild animal she is
Making a long trumpet sound.

**Sheena Moody (11)**
**Dallington CE Primary School**

# The Sea

The sea is a sly cat,
He is excited and hungry,
On summer days he purrs,
But when winter comes he hisses and claws the pebbles.

When it is night he is scared,
So he pounces up against the rocks,
When it is morning,
He reaches out to catch his prey.

**Hannah Anderson (9)**
**Dallington CE Primary School**

# The Sea

The sea is a panther,
It prowls forwards and pounces,
It tumbles into the shore and crashes upon the beach,
It growls and howls in the heavy jungle,
The sea moans, groans and screeches,
Independent and full after its day in the jungle,
Quiet and calm as it reaches the shore and turns
Back once more.

**Thomasin Quigley (10)**
**Dallington CE Primary School**

# Survivor

Tall buildings crashing to the ground
Like thunder crashing all around.
The sky black with ghostly smoke,
All you can see is people pushing bricks off them
And big clouds of dust.
As the wind blows, the air fills with dust
And you can't see anything but dust.

**Shannon Jeffery (9)**
**Elphinstone Community School**

## The Great Fire

I could see the burning buildings in the distance
They look like ancient skeletons standing on the broken roads.
I could see the thick black smoke swirling
Round me like a tornado.
I was feeling so sick not knowing
What had happened to the buildings.
Then I looked round and I saw
Empty shells that were once buildings.
I started to walk.
I walked through piles of debris and metal.
The metal was scorching hot.
I hope this was all a dream.
As I stared at the cars that were parked behind bars,
I saw standing behind the cars, charred buildings.
It felt like I had been walking for miles and miles.
As I looked around I saw burnt buildings
I could now remember what I saw
I remember seeing a big fireball
And I heard people screaming.

Karis Nash
**Elphinstone Community School**

## Football

Football comes again when it is autumn.
We all shout, 'Hooray, hooray, hooray!'
It is the best of the rest of the sports.

Football, football, comes again,
We are all loving it all day long.
We never cry if we fall over when we play football,
We just get up if we fall over.

Some support red and maybe support green and maybe support blue
And it is England and Chelsea and Man U and Arsenal!

Katriana Booth
**Elphinstone Community School**

# The Lonely City!

I'm lying on the floor,
There's something left, just a crooked door.
The city fell before my sparkly eyes
I guess it's just goodbyes
The haunted china doll lay there beside me
Now that's all I see, staring at me.
So then I shout – *'Hello!'*
But all I hear is my echo. . .
So I think I'm going to. . .
*Die!*

The village has once again been crushed
By the evil haunted china doll. . .
Let's hope it doesn't happen again!
Or will they haunt. . .
*Me!*

**Karina Golombovska**
**Elphinstone Community School**

# A Butterfly Poem

I flap my wings all day long
Until I say I want to sing a song
I'm a butterfly by the way
I like to fly until the sky's gone grey
I live in a tree and I dance with glee
So that's why I live in a tree
I love to dance with some honeybees
I do that till half-past two
So why do I dance?
I haven't got a clue
I just do it for fun
I feel so cool because I'm by a pool
Because I love to be so cool.

**Olivia Ashcroft (10)**
**Elphinstone Community School**

## Football

Football, football is so cool.
There's so many players in Arsenal.
You run up and kick a round ball.
You play and you work as a team.
Arsenal is so better than the rest.
Eleven people play on the pitch and they're the best.

Football, football is so cool.
Play in the autumn.
Arsenal they're the best.
They're good to watch on TV.
You pass when you play.

Go on Arsenal!
You're the best!

You know you rock!

**Lakeisha Ndlovu (10)**
**Elphinstone Community School**

## Autumn

Ants come out of their homes and start to sing
Along with the living things
Around them all start to grow
And grow and grow taller
Smarter, bigger and soon even kinder
The plants start to die
The leaves fall off the trees and start to crisp
As we stomp on the leaves, listen for the crunch.
I like that sound
What is that mountain doing I wonder
I know it's cold like me
You need a coat on but what does all of this mean
It's autumn.

**Katie May Verity (10)**
**Elphinstone Community School**

# Autumn

Autumn, autumn, here it comes
Crispy leaves and brown ones
Sky is grey
Coats are on
Cold is here
It carries on.
Hallowe'en's here and witches are near
Cauldrons up and bonfires struck.

Animals hibernate day by day
Different smells that make them stay.

Kids playing football out in the park
Piles of leaves stopping their league.

**Rhys Seetaram (11)**
**Elphinstone Community School**

# Autumn

Autumn, autumn, here it is
The leaves turn brown
The ground gets wet and days get shorter.
The air gets colder
The sky gets greyer
And the flowers start to die.

Bonfires get lit
Fireworks explode
The smoke looks like clouds.
Thick woolly coats go over your bodies
Like big polar bears
As rain keeps coming.

**Joshua Clarie Jocham (9)**
**Elphinstone Community School**

## Autumn

Autumn, autumn, smells like a
Fresh juicy apple.
The leaves are crispy,
Brown, red leaves as this autumn comes.
The Hallowe'en comes closer.
It's darker mornings and nights.
The frost crisps the grass as it grows.
It all hibernates
As everyone puts their coats on as bonfires glow.
The clocks turn as cold freezes every day.
The day is grey as autumn comes.
Autumn is here.

Charlie Barnett (11)
**Elphinstone Community School**

## Alone In The Deep Dark City

The whole world has collapsed right before my eyes,
Leaving me there all alone at the latest times. . .
All scared and stressed, all mad and messed
Then I think where's my beloved family
What are they doing at this time of night?
Are they asleep or even worrying about me?
Then I get it, I get it real good, I know now.
They're in a place, a place I can't go right now.
Then I shout, 'Hello, hello,' but now I know
That I will only hear my echo.
So now I know and always should have known
I'm alone in this deep, dark, dead city.

Emily Machin
**Elphinstone Community School**

## Drawing

Drawing, drawing, what good fun.
The thing we do when we're so, so bored.
You can draw fantasy.
That's why it's such fun.

It's the best thing to do with a pen or pencil.
Don't you agree?
Without drawing we cannot design buildings,
Schools, houses or supermarkets.

It doesn't matter what you draw.
It's all your imagination that you can draw.

**Benjamin Newman (11)**
**Elphinstone Community School**

## Ruined City

I can see the misty dust
In freezing cold air.
The crushed up buildings were crumbling
Very slowly.
I could smell the burning smoke
In the dusty and misty air.
I could see the amber lights
Shining through the broken windows.
I was just at the towers
And they were as black as coal.

**Aaron James (9)**
**Elphinstone Community School**

## The Dark Day

The whole world has collapsed before me,
Leaving me alone at night . . .
All scared and stressed, all mad and messed.
Then I think - *where's my family?*
Then I get my answer.
They're somewhere I cannot go yet.
Then I shout - 'Hello?'
All I hear is my echo . . .
So now I know.
I'm alone in this unspirited, dead city . . .

Nayla Mauthoor (9)
**Elphinstone Community School**

## Survivor

I woke up in shock.
I couldn't move at all.
My leg was in pain.
When I managed to move
I looked out the damaged window to see what was going on.
Once I saw it I ran to the phone. . .
It didn't work, I felt so depressed.
I sat down and thought and thought and thought.

Jessica Wilmshurst
**Elphinstone Community School**

## Untitled

Rumbling buildings, tatty roads dirty as dust.
Grey, mysterious smoke coming from nowhere.
The bright orange sky gazing at the tall smoky towers.
Crooked church leaning against the blackened sky with fading dust.

Katarina Reed
**Elphinstone Community School**

# Ruined City

I could see the misty dust in the freezing cold air.
I could smell the burning smoke
In the dusty and misty air.
The crushed up buildings were crumbling.

**Troi Burnett**
**Elphinstone Community School**

# The Burning City

I can see an old crooked church
I can smell smoke coming from a house
I can see a bright orange and yellow light
And I can smell burning.

**Olivia Ruff (10)**
**Elphinstone Community School**

# Parasite

I see the once epic city is now a home for monsters
Who shelter in the ragged building.
The whole things starts when mysterious green gas
Came and burned everything in existence.

**Kieran John**
**Elphinstone Community School**

# The Unknown City

The mysterious buildings.
Were crumbling down like shattered skeletons.
So bleeding souls and bleeding people.
So now I am dead.

**Kelis Kenefeck**
**Elphinstone Community School**

## In the Dark, Spooky Cave

I had an uncomfortable mattress.
I didn't like it because it was bumpy,
But I used it for a midnight bed.
I'd got creamy wax melted to make flaming candles
At the side of the dark cave,
Also a dirty, creased net for a bed cover.
It was hanging from the cave.
There was another net, it was under my freezing feet.
Wet, crumbly sweet wrappers for beautiful designs like wallpaper
Were in the corner of the damp cave.
Dirty, stuffed, old cushions for a comfy sofa
Were sticking on the cave because it was wet!
I collected sparkly diamonds for a great wallpaper
Like sweet wrappers.
All the things I collected from the dark, spooky cave I left there,
But I made it like I wanted it to be!

Aminah Rahman (8)
**Estcots Primary School**

## In My Cave

In the pool of the cave salty ripples appeared
In the centre of the dirty water.
A round plastic tray for a plate was lying on the floor
Along with a pile of round rocks.
I collected rubies, diamonds and jewels for the walls.
I had jewellery and rings hanging from hard rocks.
A hot lantern was lit near to a box of matches
To keep me warm whilst lying in the cold night.
On the floor I buried some pyrite so I was rich.
I fixed together some smooth tree logs for a seat.
At the back were a pair of tyres
Which looked like they came from a bike.
I wonder if that day will happen again.

Lauren Mansi (7)
**Estcots Primary School**

# The Solar System

T he solar system,
H ot fireballs flying in space,
E arth is big, blue and green, swirling patches of mist surrounding it

S aturn is an orange planet,
O ur planet is Earth,
L ate to get to the rocket,
A re you coming with us?
R ockets are extremely massive!

S o, what time are we leaving?
Y ou nearly drove into a gas ball!
S un, sun, sun,
T he sun is the closest,
E arth is the best!
M y goodness, I'm on the moon!

**Amy Gunn (9)**
**Estcots Primary School**

# Planets

The planets are magical,
Aliens are real,
Go into space,
And you'll become a meal.

Jupiter is enormous,
Mercury is tiny,
Uranus is on its side
And Neptune looks slimy.

The sun is bad
To look at through your eyes,
When you get out of space,
You'd better eat some pies!

**Sachin Bhangra (9)**
**Estcots Primary School**

## The Bright Sun

T he sun is bright,
H e wanted to see it,
E arth is our planet,

B etter than ever,
R ed hot gas,
I am scared about going to the stars,
G oing to the bright stars,
H ere I come!
T o the moon we go!

S o, are you scared?
U p to space we go,
N ever going to forget it.

**Leah Harris (9)**
**Estcots Primary School**

## The Milky Way

T he Milky Way
H igh in the sky
E ager to go up there and see

M iles to go
I can't wait!
L ift off!
K ey to the stars
Y ay!

W here is it?
A lmost there
Y ippee! We have arrived!

**Antonia Major (9)**
**Estcots Primary School**

# Snow Spider

S now spider
N ot to be seen by anyone else
O ut of this world!
W onderfully white

S ilver and special
P retty and sweet
I ncredibly cute
D elicate
E xtraordinary
R emarkable!

**Jordan Crowther (9)**
**Estcots Primary School**


# In My Dusty Cave

In the dusty corner of the cave I would store my bed made of cardboard boxes, then a lumpy mattress on top.
At the back of the cave I would put broken chairs with a table to eat my cooked meals.
On the ceiling there were frightening, fluffy bats.
Below my feet there were bashed up bits of glass to shine to make light.
At the side of the cave I would keep snapped bookshelves to keep my books on.
Then I wondered and hoped if I would get home again.

**Molly Walter (8)**
**Estcots Primary School**


# Untitled

If I lived in a cave I would have a chair made of wood and felt.
If I lived in a cave I would have an old bed made out of straw.
If I lived in a cave I would have a ripped, grey, smelly sofa.

**Catalina Fernandez (8) & Jak Kettley (7)**
**Estcots Primary School**

## What Would I Use?

My cave is creepy.
In the back there are some old, crusty little poles with a blanket on top.
In the corner of my cave there is a small tin can for a rubbish bin
And at the centre of my dark, creepy cave there is a bunch of old, black, dirty tyres and some torn newspaper too.
At the entrance of my cave there is a hot, yellow fire burning with sticks as well.
And at the side of my wet cave there are cushions and a ragged newspaper for a comfy sofa.

Sorcha Parker Thompson (7)
**Estcots Primary School**

## The Cold Cave

Above my head I could feel tickly creepers.
I could see in the back of the cave two dirty sticks to make a fire with.
In the spookiest part of the cave I could cut sharp flint, it was so prickly.
Old sweet wrappers to wrap up presents.
Shiny smooth pyrite in the walls.
Soft cushions to lie on.
Brown, old tree trunk to eat my food on.
Water bottle for a telephone and some string to talk through.

Reid Jenden (8)
**Estcots Primary School**

## If I Lived

If I lived in a cave I would have a comfy chair made of silk and wood
If I lived in a cave I would have a bed made of wood and wool
If I lived in a cave I would have a table made out of wood
And a bowl made out of glass
If I lived in a cave I would have a big teddy bear.

Kieran Taylor (8) & Erin Reakes (7)
**Estcots Primary School**

## In My Cave

In the corner of the dark, black cave I felt hard, rusty rocks on my feet.
On the side of the dusty cave I could see old, screwed up newspapers.
In the back of the scary, freaky cave I could see dry sticks to make a burning hot fire.
On the bumpy floor of the cave I saw wet, colourful stones.
In the back of the scary cave I could smell sweet, colourful wrappers.

Jasmine Prior (7)
**Estcots Primary School**

## Untitled

If I lived in a cave I would have a mobile made out of wood and leaves.
If I lived in a cave I would have a bed made out of wool and old wood.
If I lived in a cave I would have a teddy made out of wool with a button eye.
If I lived in a cave I would have a window made out of wood.
If I lived in a cave I would have a football made from old tin foil.

Jade Edgar & Emelia Aylmer (7)
**Estcots Primary School**

## Untitled

By the creepy entrance of the dark, spooky cave,
I saw old, broken car doors and an old bike with no wheels
And the handles as bars.
Old, smelly, holey wellies,
Old, red, melted wax to make old, dusty candles
To light up the cave.
Then I found some dry sticks to make a fire
To warm me up in the cold cave at night.

Connor Lunn (8)
**Estcots Primary School**

## The Snow Spider

The snow spider's back, oh so swirly
The snow spider's web, oh so curvy
The snow spiders can be all different sizes
The snow spiders can bring all different surprises
The snow spider's legs, oh so long
The snow spider's web, oh so strong
The snow spider's body, oh so thin
The snow spider can spin a web like anything.

Chloe Robinson (9)
**Estcots Primary School**

## My Dark Cave

At the side of my cave I'd put a mattress with a wrinkly cushion for a bed.
Sticks and stones to make patterns and a fire at the back of the cave.
In the middle of the cave I would put old, broken china cups to drink from.
I went to sleep. It was very cold so I was shivering.

Jack Gentry (7)
**Estcots Primary School**

## The Mysterious Cave

In the gloomy middle of the cave
I had wax melted to make flaming,
Dazzling candles to make a fire.
At the entrance of the cave
I would have wet stones to make a pattern.
On the bottom of the cave
I would have a smelly rug.

Christopher Leroy (7)
**Estcots Primary School**

# The Magic Cave

Above me I see a tyre and string for a swing.
In the dark corner I see a ladder for a bed.
On the left-hand side I have some soft, fluffy, puffy, pink cushions.

Next to my bed I have some string and a cup for a mobile.
In the back of my cave I can see diamonds in the wall of the cave.
On the right-hand side I see lit candles on the table.

Danica Proctor (8)
**Estcots Primary School**

# In My Wonderful Cave

In the middle were old tables and chairs.
In the corner I could see leaves for making cushions.
In the middle there were metal tins for making telephones.
Dusty wax melted to make warm candles.
To the side were old mattresses for my bed.
Wonderful fools' gold in the walls made the walls glittery.

Rosie Jane Sands (7)
**Estcots Primary School**

# My Cave

In the spookiest part of the cave there was a bit of sharp flint
To cut bits of smooth rock to make a bed,
Some long creepers to hang some clothes on.
In the corner there were some old, sharp sticks to make fire.
At the side there was some metal to make a chair.
In the middle there was some fur to make a bag.

Brice Major (7)
**Estcots Primary School**

## Untitled

If I lived in a cave I would have an old, rusty bed with smelly coats.
If I lived in a cave I would have a brown, ripped sofa.
If I lived in a cave I would have a scruffy bed made out of wood and wool.
If I lived in a cave I would have a red chair made out of rusty metal and a pink, smelly pillow.

**Mary Haines (8) & Sian Fuller (7)**
Estcots Primary School

## Untitled

If I lived in a cave I would have a fluffy teddy made out of cotton wool.
If I lived in a cave I would have a broken sofa.
If I lived in a cave I would have a ball made out of string.
If I lived in a cave I would have a table made out of wood and stone.
If I lived in a cave I would have an old football made out of tin foil.

**Sophie Parsonage & Nathan Robinson (7)**
Estcots Primary School

## Untitled

If I lived in a cave I would have a very big ball so I could play with it.
If I lived in a cave I would have an old, dirty, plastic, grey bottle to drink from.
If I lived in a cave I would have a red bicycle.
If I lived in a cave I would have a table made from stacked, hard, black tyres.

**Thomas Oomen & Melek Gunes (8)**
Estcots Primary School

# The Dark Cave

In the corner of the cave it was spooky and dark.
There was a bike and under it was a sharp flint for a fire,
But it was broken.
Then I saw hanging from the roof, a candle for a boot lace.
It was old, it had been there for years.
On a seat of cushions I was comfy.

**Lewis Holmes (7)**
**Estcots Primary School**

# Untitled

In the ceiling I could see flint shining up above.
In the spooky, dark, wet, damp corner I could see sharp fools' gold.
When I walked forwards into the cave, I noticed that my cave was made out of marble.
There was Lego and baby chairs.
Bricks and blocks had fallen from the cave.

**Thomas Searle (7)**
**Estcots Primary School**

# Untitled

If I lived in a cave I would have a bunk bed with grass
If I lived in a cave I would have a big book
If I lived in a cave I would have a fluffy teddy
He has a little missing eye
He is made out of cotton wool
If I lived in a cave I would have an old book with ripped pages.

**Dillon Stahl & Jemma Edgar (7)**
**Estcots Primary School**

## Untitled

In the shadow of my cave there is a tree stump for a table.
A newspaper to put on a smooth door for a bed.
Some pillows for a sofa.
Some string and cans for a telephone.
Some dusty wax melted to make a flaming candle.
Some sticks for a fire.

Julia Nield (7)
**Estcots Primary School**

## Untitled

If I lived in a cave I would have an old bed made from wood and cotton wool.
If I lived in a cave I would have a table
If I lived in a cave I would have a window made from wood and plastic.

Jayden Brown & Sam Sloan (7)
**Estcots Primary School**

## In The Shadowy Mouth

I saw pyrite like the sun.
I picked up some pyrite.
I went to the shadowy corner.
I saw old, broken newspaper for a bed to sleep on.

Ben Mooney (8)
**Estcots Primary School**

## By The Dark Rock At The Entrance

In my dark cave I would have dry old wood for a fire.
On a little shelf I would have red wax melted to make new candles.
In the walls I would have sparkly marble.

Adam Stevens (7)
**Estcots Primary School**

# Untitled

If I lived in a cave I would make a TV out of plastic with smelly hay
If I lived in a cave I would have a table made out of wood
If I lived in a cave I would have a rusty old bed
If I lived in a cave I would have a fluffy hamster.

**Reece Jell & Tom Wallis (7)**
Estcots Primary School

# Untitled

If I lived in a cave I would have my soft teddy bear
If I lived in a cave I would have my red toy car
If I lived in a cave I would have a teddy made out of fluff
and cotton wool.

**Aaron Wareing (7) & Niall Moloney (8)**
Estcots Primary School

# My Dark Cave

By the entrance in the walls there was glittery pyrite.
I was using old newspaper as a bed in the shadowed corner.
Next I went to the left corner.
I used an old, smooth tree stump for a chair.

**Amy Lopez (7)**
Estcots Primary School

# My Secret Cave

In the middle of my cave, lying under my feet,
I can see a smooth door to make a brilliant bed.
At the back of the cave I have some fresh food and water.
Above my head I can see some black bats to scare people away.

**Matthew Tomkinson (7)**
Estcots Primary School

## A List Of Tiny, Funny Stuff

How happy -
When you
Find some
Pie on the
Table
Unguarded.

How happy -
When you get
That first
Smell of
The day.

How happy -
When you
Shout but
No one
Argues.

How happy -
When you
See your pet
Curled up
In a ball.

How happy -
When you
Jump on
The trampoline
And fall back
Down.

How happy -
When you
Find your
Way round
Your house
With your
Eyes closed.

**Drew Castle (9)**
**Ninfield CE Primary School**

# A Delightful Poem

How happy -
When it's Easter
And when you take your first
Bite of a fresh, hard chocolate egg.

How happy -
When you discover
Some money behind the brown bookshelf
Though it's been hijacked
By grey dust.

How happy -
When you
Walk along the soft, sandy beach
And the waves crash heavily
Onto the hard rocks.

How happy -
When you
Get a gorgeous white
Butterfly on your
Finger.

How happy -
When you skip
So quickly the air
In you disappears.

How happy -
When you discover
How to lick the
Tip of your nose.

**Rebekah Hesmer (9)**
**Ninfield CE Primary School**

## A List Of Small And Mostly Happy Things

How happy -
When you take the first bite
Of a delicious
Crunchy pizza.

How happy -
When you discover
Your DS down the side of the sofa
Despite the dirty dust.

How happy -
When you get a house point
For your work
Twice in a row.

How happy -
When you see a blackbird
Lay a black
Speckled egg.

How happy -
When you
Run outside in the snow
And build a snowman.

How sad -
When your dog dies
And it's only
One year old.

**Fallon Scott (9)**
**Ninfield CE Primary School**

## My Amazing Moods

How happy -
When you take
Your first delightful crunch
On a delicious, creamy meringue
And daydream.

How happy -
When you discover
That your sweet, silly dog
Has locked itself outside
The glass doors.

How happy -
When you get the chance
To make chocolate chip
Fudge cake, your favourite.

How happy -
When you see
A beautiful white butterfly
Spring up into the
Clear blue sky.

How disappointed -
When you find out
That a part of a lifetime
Has been cancelled.

**Charlotte Packham (9)**
**Ninfield CE Primary School**

## Firm Feelings

How happy -
When you grasp
An extra long
Lie in on a
Saturday.

How gratified -
When you bag
The first place
Medal like a hero.

How lonely -
When all your
Companions
Go in for tea.

How surprised -
When your
Friends prepare
A surprise party.

How disappointed -
When you find
Out this is
Only a dream.

**Kieran Hook (9)**
**Ninfield CE Primary School**

# My Emotions

How happy
When you suck
The oozing cheese
Off a pizza.

How sad
When you walk slowly
Towards your closest
Friend's funeral.

How scared
When you hear crackling
When you are alone in a
Wood at night.

How ecstatic
When you discover
A cute, cuddly kitten
In your cat's basket.

How proud
When you earn
A massive medal
As shiny as a fresh cut diamond.

**Katie Styles (9)**
**Ninfield CE Primary School**

*Poetry Explorers 2009 - Sussex*

## How

How happy -
When you see
A brown squirrel
Jumping tree to tree.

How disappointed -
When you discover
Your cat can't
Have kittens.

How excited -
When you find out
You've
Won the lottery.

How thrilled -
When the
Hot summer
Finally comes.

How brave -
When the shutters
Go *bang!*
In the night.

**Josie Stickells (10)**
**Ninfield CE Primary School**

# My Amazing Moods

How proud -
I am when I
Find a five pound note
Hidden down the back of the sofa.

How sad -
When my best friend
Moves to a different school
And doesn't say goodbye.

How annoying -
When you buy a sweet
And only get the wrapper
But don't get your money back.

How happy -
When you sip the last mouthful
Of your favourite drink
Then find more in the cupboard.

How embarrassing -
When you go to lick your lolly
Then it falls to the floor
And everyone laughs at you.

Molly Butler (10)
**Ninfield CE Primary School**

## My Moods

How happy -
When you take
The first lick
Of a fizzy lollipop.

How happy -
When you find
One sweet in a secret
Sweet tin.

How happy -
When you go
Down the bike ramp
And the wind catches your hair.

How happy -
When you get
To the beginning
Of the school holidays.

How scary -
When you walk
Through hospital doors.

**Nathan Creasey (9)**
**Ninfield CE Primary School**

# A Small List Of My Feelings

How happy -
When you take
That first mouthful of delicious
Mint chocolate chip ice cream
And shiver.

How excited -
When you discover
A ten pound note in the gutter
Even though it is covered in stinky sewage.

How brave -
When you finally
Have the guts
To abseil down
A ginormous cliff.

How happy -
When you find out
That you can
Touch your nose
With your tongue.

**Isabelle Corby (9)**
**Ninfield CE Primary School**

Poetry Explorers 2009 - Sussex

## You Are Happy When . . .

How happy -
When you have the first
Bite of juicy burger
And can't stop.

How happy -
When you find money
Outside a shop.

How happy -
When it's the
School holidays
And no homework.

How happy -
When there's a school trip
To a chocolate factory.

How happy -
When you discover
You can lick your nose.

**Daniel Abel (10)**
**Ninfield CE Primary School**

# My Feelings

How happy -
When I find a
Packet of my favourite
Crisps even though
They are a year out of date.

How excited -
When I am watching
The lottery with a gleaming
Ticket in my hand.

How embarrassed -
When I fall
Off my motorbike
In front of a crowd.

How hungry -
When I get a
Whiff of fresh
Smooth chocolate.

**Jonathan Masters (9)**
**Ninfield CE Primary School**

*Poetry Explorers 2009 - Sussex*

## Mixed Emotions On The Pitch

How happy -
When you return
From a football match
And smell roast dinner.

How jolly -
When you discover
A sauna in the away team
Changing room.

How embarrassed -
When you miss
An open goal in a
Crowded stadium.

How proud -
When you hit
The top corner
From twenty yards.

**James Kildea (9)**
**Ninfield CE Primary School**

## The Seaside

I can hear the sea crashing against the pebbles to make a smooth harmony.
I can see the seagulls flying high in the air and swooping down into the water hoping to catch a fish.
I can smell the sea salt in the air going into your nose and just staying there.
I can taste my nice, soft ice cream keeping me cool from the blazing sun.
I can touch a crab, washed up by the tide, be careful with his pincers or he will make you cry.
I like the beach, it is like home, except for the water and for the stones, but people make it more like home.

Lewis Remmer (10)
**SS Peter & Paul CE Primary School, Bexhill-on-Sea**

# On The Beach

On the beach, I am kneeling on the soft sand,
I can feel the jagged, shattered mussel shell
Drilling its sharp corners into my fingers,
The cool breeze blowing against my face, soothingly.

On the beach, I am sitting on the smooth, round stones,
I can hear the waves of the immense blue sea
Crashing furiously against the rocks,
The cries of a lonely seagull, calling for company.

On the beach, I am lying peacefully,
Staring longingly at the cloudless sky,
I am blinded by the fiery sun beaming on the ripples of the calm sea,
Seagulls circling and squawking above my head.

On the beach I am running frantically towards the ocean,
I can smell the salty, fishy essence entering the cave of my nose,
The sweet scent of delicious hot dogs cooking in the distance.

On the beach, I am jumping excitedly
Over the freezing waves of the sapphire sea.
I can taste the cold, bitter air seeping into my mouth,
The soft ice cream with its heavenly sweetness melting on my tongue.

On the concrete, I am climbing up the mountainous ramp,
I can hear children laughing and screaming,
See the café across the busy road,
Smell the gas from the cars passing by,
Taste the crunchy cone of my ice cream
Until I am on the beach no more.

Ayesha Shrestha (10)
**SS Peter & Paul CE Primary School, Bexhill-on-Sea**

*Poetry Explorers 2009 - Sussex*

## The Trip To The Beach

Since I started Year 6,
I was looking forward to this.
A trip to the beach,
Oh yes, we go,
I just wish the tide is low.
I know it travels to and fro,
I really do wish the tide is low.
Seagulls squawking all the time,
Calling for their friends they are.
I could smell the fish and chips,
One of my favourite foods that is!
Smelling ice cream wafting in the air
And feeling the wind brushing my hair.
A real live crab,
That's what I saw.
The stones crunching under my feet,
While I watch the old people eat.
The sea is getting rougher now,
The sailing boats go up and down.
I wish I could go again,
I've got to go,
Bye-bye then.

Alexandra Lazarova (10)
**SS Peter & Paul CE Primary School, Bexhill-on-Sea**

## Bexhill Beach

Add the crashing of the sea fighting with the rocks,
Mix the fingerprints of the ocean underneath my legs,
Whisk in the silky smooth texture of the sweet, cold ice cream,
Pour in the sea creatures, some dead and some alive.
Sprinkle the savage seagulls hunting the weak and helpless,
Stir the salt into the rattling winds and the scent of the fish
Stagnant and polluted, but at the same time natural and clean.
A beach is born!

Jade Walker (10)
**SS Peter & Paul CE Primary School, Bexhill-on-Sea**

## The Beach

Whistling wind in my dark brown hair,
The warm breeze softly caressing my face,
I scan the ground for shells,
Some used by hermit crabs, some just empty of life.
The clinging crabs settling under the rough rocks.
Crawling around we sit listening, watching,
Waiting for the next wave to come crashing down.
Hearing the sound of rattling stones pulled to and fro by the waves,
Staggering up the roller coaster of curious pebbles,
I find a medley of shells, seaweed, cuttlefish bones,
Bottle tops, old shoe soles.
The smooth taste of the salty sea air,
The stinging smell of fish tickling my nostrils.
*Crash!* go the pebbles as I walk, being bullied by the tide.
Staring at the sky,
Reflected in the sapphire, shimmering sea.
Fluffy, white clouds hover above,
Fluttering overhead the squawking hunt for food.
The perfect beach.

Matthew Payne (10)
**SS Peter & Paul CE Primary School, Bexhill-on-Sea**

## The Beach Senses

I can taste the coolness of the breeze rushing through my mouth,
It's all fresh and clean.
I can taste a milky mix from my ice cream!
I can smell a tang from the sea, swiftly drifting all around.
I can smell salt from a fish and chip shop.
I can hear crashing against the rocks coming up to shore.
I can hear the crushing of a mussel shell under a foot!
I can see the sun glistening on the sea.
I can see Beachy Head on the horizon.
I can feel a rippled seashell under my back.
I feel the breeze swirling around me.

India Gomes (10)
**SS Peter & Paul CE Primary School, Bexhill-on-Sea**

*Poetry Explorers 2009 - Sussex*

## Our Beach Trip

Smelling the slimy seaweed, wanting to walk on the beach
I love going to the beach
Hearing the beautiful waves crash against the hard, dangerous rocks
Feeling the stumpy rocks whilst sitting down
Seeing the seagulls calling a troop of other seagulls squawking their beaks off
While wanting to go in the sea, the teacher tells my group we can go and get an ice cream, *mmm,* so yum and scrum
Closing my eyes, feeling the wind pass me, liking the sound
The wind gets stronger, feeling so cool
Now I am doing a treasure hunt
Walking on the sand feeling disgusted because it is so yucky
My eye caught a crab - what we need for the hunt - it was so horrible, the crab
Finding a starfish - where is it? My group looks everywhere
A beautiful summer breeze fills the air
People's hair feels the air while it is blowing
The rocks are going and we are leaving, bye-bye and now I have done.

Asia Hadleigh (10)
**SS Peter & Paul CE Primary School, Bexhill-on-Sea**

## The Seaside

Add the rough stones
Then mix in the salty, calm sea.
Sprinkle the gold, thick sand
To make a beautiful mixture
And to make it light and fluffy.
Whip in the cool breeze.
Pour in the sealife to liven things up.
Whisk for about twenty minutes.
As your dish develops
You will start to smell the salty tang
And taste the freshness.

Reece Sorrell (10)
**SS Peter & Paul CE Primary School, Bexhill-on-Sea**

# I See

I see big waves,
I see small waves,
I see the light reflecting on the sea,
I see the water trying to get to the sea under the rocks,
I see rock pools all around,
I smell the lovely smell of the seaside,
I smell fish from the sea,
I can taste salt from the sea,
I can taste fresh air,
I feel well,
I feel relaxed,
I can touch sharp rocks,
I can touch the nice shells,
I can touch the wet sand,
I can hear the seagulls,
I can hear the waves,
I can hear the teachers talking,
*I like it at the seaside!*

**Lily Clough (10)**
**SS Peter & Paul CE Primary School, Bexhill-on-Sea**

# Seaside Blend

Add the soft sand and crunching pebbles,
Sprinkle the smooth rocks and mix in the crumbling crabs,
Pour in the glittering sea,
Crack the tangy salt air then shake the smell of the fish and sea,
Whisk in the puffy, white clouds and a handful of gentle breeze,
Then add the beaming heat and the smooth, slimy starfish,
Take a pinch of sound - the crackle of the stones
Like the autumn leaves you walk on
And the whisper of the wind just gently passing by.
Stir a tablespoon of fresh air and salt for taste,
Lastly add a beach hut for a treat and then just you and me.
Relax!

**Amy Streets (10)**
**SS Peter & Paul CE Primary School, Bexhill-on-Sea**

*Poetry Explorers 2009 - Sussex*

## My Day At The Beach

To the beach many times I've been, but I have never seen . . .
The seagulls flying to and fro calling to their friends,
The pebbles being washed up on the beach,
The rough rocks shining in the sun,
The sun shining on my face.

To the beach many times I've been, but I have never felt . . .
The stones in my hands, all different shapes and sizes,
The hot sun on my face.

To the beach many times I've been, but I have never heard . . .
The crashing of the angry waves,
People's footsteps on the stones.

To the beach many times I've been, but I have never smelt . . .
The salty air from the sea,
The salty seaweed.

To the beach many times I've been, but I have never tasted . . .
The fresh, salty air in my mouth.

**Katy Hannah (10)**
**SS Peter & Paul CE Primary School, Bexhill-on-Sea**

## The Seaside

The seawater on the seashore,
Rushing through the rocks,
A big wave coming towards us,
Run, run from the big sea,
The wind blowing on my face,
A lovely breeze it was,
I could hear the pebbles crunching,
Underneath my feet,
The seagulls squawking in the sky,
I see lots of stones,
I can smell and taste salt when I take a breath.

**Karafa-Jasmine Janneh (10)**
**SS Peter & Paul CE Primary School, Bexhill-on-Sea**

## The Sea's Secrets

I can feel the pebbles under my feet while the wind is on my face
As cold as ever.
The ice cream on my lips that came from the seaside shop.
I can see children playing on the beach and pebbles and shells
Below me.
Watching the waves crashing on the rocks, I feel as if I'm moving
In the gentle gust of wind.
I can taste the smooth ice cream on my lips.
When I breathe in, I can taste the saltiness of the sea on my tongue.
I can smell interesting smells from the seaside shop.
The smell of salt on my nose, like it will never go away.
I can hear seagulls above me calling to their friends,
Children calling and screaming as they run away from the sea as it
Very nearly gets them.
Cars go by behind me like sounds from a video game.
I like the sound of the wind on the tops of bottles, *oooh* they go.

**Hannah Honeysett-Skippings (10)**
**SS Peter & Paul CE Primary School, Bexhill-on-Sea**

## My Relaxing Day

First add the silky, golden sand
With the whooshing of the wind
Along with the hard, crunchy pebbles,
And mix them up with the sharp, crystal rocks.
Then add the dazzling sun
And the fluffy clouds.
After that, add the rough, wavy waves
With the darting little fish,
The snappy crabs,
The rough, orange starfish,
The slimy rock pools
And the sticky, hard mussels.
Then finally, the sound of the yummy ice cream
And the white, singing seagulls.

**Chloe Whiting (10)**
**SS Peter & Paul CE Primary School, Bexhill-on-Sea**

*Poetry Explorers 2009 - Sussex*

## The Seaside

Mix in the tangy sea smell with the smooth, curious pebbles
And sprinkle the wet, crystal-like sand into the salty mixture,
Then whisk for 7 minutes.
Try to catch the chilly breeze of a cold day at the beach,
Pour it carefully and gently into the mixture
And carry on stirring for a few more minutes.
Collect the bits of driftwood that are lying across the beach
And add to your mixture.
Grab the seagulls' cries and stir them carefully
To give an extra boost of energy and surround sound.
Then get some fresh fish and blend into the shimmering sea
Along with an amazing collection of sealife -
Crabs, octopus, sharks, dolphins and starfish.
Then bake for 20 minutes.
When it is finished cooking, there you have your very own beach.

Lucy Swatton (10)
**SS Peter & Paul CE Primary School, Bexhill-on-Sea**

## A Trip To The Beach

The sea crashing against the wall of shingle.
The birds calling from one housetop to the other.
The whistling of the bitter wind.
As the winds blow in my face
I can feel the ocean spray and taste the tangy sea salt.
Looking out at the musty sea and the shell-covered groynes
And landscape, I feel in a trance.
Nothing could be more magical.
Then the adventure stops.
All I can hear are the impatient people waiting for the ice cream
That seems to remedy the hotness.
But it's alright because we're sitting on the beach
With an ice cream each and I'm happy.

Kiziah Lloyd-Graham (10)
**SS Peter & Paul CE Primary School, Bexhill-on-Sea**

## Lovely Beach Rhythm

On the stormy seas,
With rocking boats,
Seagulls roar through the air.

The rushing ocean carries boats away
And the running wind blows through my hair,
Delivering the pebbles
And the sea creatures to the beach.

Pour the salty sea into the ocean
And the ice cream on my tongue,
As I sit with hard rocks to cushion my backside.

**Ben Chervi (10)**
**SS Peter & Paul CE Primary School, Bexhill-on-Sea**

# The Beach

As I feel the wind brush against my face,
I lick ice cream away from my chin
And listen to the cheerful voices of people strolling by.

The seagulls squawk above me,
The water caresses the rocks
And I stare out, over the crystal clear water
To Beachy Head,
Over the shimmering waves
And far, far away!

**Chloe Jennings-Weir (10)**
**SS Peter & Paul CE Primary School, Bexhill-on-Sea**

# The Seaside

I can feel the pebbles crunching under my feet,
Then the sun shining on my back,
The sun glistening on the ocean blue as seagulls flew
Through the sparkle of the sun, squawking for fun.

**Hayden Fox (10)**
**SS Peter & Paul CE Primary School, Bexhill-on-Sea**

*Poetry Explorers 2009 - Sussex*

## Beach Recipe

Add in the silky, smooth pebbles that are warm.
Include the hot, golden, soft and shiny sand.
Mix in the rugged, brown and grey seaweed-covered rocks
And create crater-like rock pools.
Stir the immense, blue sea that crashes on the rocks.
Into the sea sprinkle a multitude of tiny and mammoth,
Pretty and alien-like sea creatures to play in the sea.
Whisk it all up with some crunchy shells
And bake in the beautiful golden sun.

**Rebecca Palmer (10)**
SS Peter & Paul CE Primary School, Bexhill-on-Sea

## Down At The Seaside

Firstly add slime of the rocks then
Carefully pour the crispy stones in.
Add the sticky sand and whisk carefully.
Take a big breath of the fresh, crisp air, then mix.
Next add the candyfloss clouds,
Stir the mixture with a whole bucketful of icy sea water.
Take the music from the ice cream van
And cook it all for twenty minutes,
Then you are ready to serve your seaside dish.

**Ryan Blackford (10)**
SS Peter & Paul CE Primary School, Bexhill-on-Sea

## The Calm Beach

Add the sand and the soft pebbles
Mix the fish into the shimmering sea
And the shining sun
Sprinkle on the magical salt water
Pour the silky sand mix in the boats on the waves
Whisk in some singing seagulls and pour into the ocean.

**Simona Shaji (10)**
SS Peter & Paul CE Primary School, Bexhill-on-Sea

# The Beach

As I heard the pebbles crunching under my feet.
As I heard the burst of laughter, as I heard the buzz of aeroplanes.
As I smelt the warm fish.
As I heard the seagulls squawking to one another.
As I tasted my scrummy, cold ice cream, I heard the waves crashing against the rough rocks.
As I walked along the pebbles, I felt the rough pebbles against my soft hand.
As I walked home I thought how lucky I am!

Francesca Huff (10)
**SS Peter & Paul CE Primary School, Bexhill-on-Sea**

# Wild Beach Trip

Shimmering reflection,
As sparkly as a mirror,
The sea smooth and calm
Yet powerful as it fights
With the rocks,
Pebbles dragged back by the waves,
Watch the sparkle from the sun
Reflecting off the shiny, blue ocean.

Connor Porthouse (10)
**SS Peter & Paul CE Primary School, Bexhill-on-Sea**

# Max's Beach Trip

As I was blinded by the dazzling sun
I licked my ice cream away from my chin
The salty air tickled my nostrils
And the stench of dead fish drifted up my nose
I felt the rocks smooth and cold between my toes
And gazed out at the magnificent ocean
Iridescent from the sun's rays.

Max Giles (10)
**SS Peter & Paul CE Primary School, Bexhill-on-Sea**

## The Seaside

I can feel the autumn breeze blowing through my hair.
I can taste the cold ice cream running down my throat,
See the big waves crashing on the groynes,
Hear the seagulls squawking up, up in the air.
I can hear the stones crashing underneath my feet.
I can see the rock pools, big and small.
Things here and things there, the sight of the seaside,
A marvellous sight to see!

Eleanor Packer (10)
SS Peter & Paul CE Primary School, Bexhill-on-Sea

## The Wonderful Sea

Listen to the sea crashing on the rock pools,
The waves dragging the pebbles back.
Feel the chill of the wind down your neck.
Watch the seagulls' feathers blowing around.
Can't you just smell the fish food,
With the water spraying in your face
With the revolting aftertaste?

Rowan Martyn (10)
SS Peter & Paul CE Primary School, Bexhill-on-Sea

## Seaside

Add the soft, silky sand,
Mix in the pebbles,
Pour in the cold, blue sea,
Crack the small fragments of seaweed,
Ice the cool breeze,
Whisk in a handful of fluffy clouds
And you have the sweet, sweet beach.

Alex Skilton (10)
SS Peter & Paul CE Primary School, Bexhill-on-Sea

## The Beach

I can hear pebbles crunching hard against my feet,
The joyful laughter bursts my ears as I sit and listen.
The buzz of aeroplanes flying low over the sea.
The salty fish taste of the ocean drifting over the world.
The spiky edges of mussel shells prick me on the leg.
I sit with my back facing the sun, it warms me.

**Nicola Galt (10)**
**SS Peter & Paul CE Primary School, Bexhill-on-Sea**

## The Sea

I could hear the wavy sea crashing
I could feel the fiery heat on my skin
I could smell the sugary ice cream
I could feel the bumpy stones
I could taste the tasty ice cream
I could smell the rotten salt.

**Alex Blatchly (10)**
**SS Peter & Paul CE Primary School, Bexhill-on-Sea**

## The Beach

Add the sand and the pebbles
Mix in the rocks
Whisk in the shells
Plant some seaweed
And place some fish in the sea
And you have a beach.

**Feaw Inplaeng (11)**
**SS Peter & Paul CE Primary School, Bexhill-on-Sea**

## Swaying Of The Sea

Once there was a boat swiftly floating,
Across the ocean sea,
But then came the wind blowing,
Across the howling sea,
But there came a man and his dog,
Trying to get out of the sandy bog.

Daniel Joseph (10)
**SS Peter & Paul CE Primary School, Bexhill-on-Sea**

## By The Seaside

I can hear the stones crunching under my feet
And feel the sun warming my back with its heat.
Joyful laughter all around
And a shattered shell which I found
And a splodge of ice cream on the ground.
A seagull that soars in the sky with delight and fun.

Jimi Cutting (10)
**SS Peter & Paul CE Primary School, Bexhill-on-Sea**

## The Seaside

First add the silky, crystal sand
And hard, crunchy pebbles
Mixing the rocks with the shimmering sea
Sprinkle a handful of fluffy clouds
And a gentle breathtaking breeze.

Brandon Beal (11)
**SS Peter & Paul CE Primary School, Bexhill-on-Sea**

## Sunny Seaside

I can hear pebbles crunching under my feet.
I feel the sun warming my back.
I see the rusty groynes as rusty as ever, the ocean blue.
I hear a seagull in the sky flying through the sparkle of the sun,
Squawking with delight and fun.

**Jason Fox (10)**
**SS Peter & Paul CE Primary School, Bexhill-on-Sea**

## The Sea

I'm not like the glistening sea, it roams free, unlike me.
For the crashing sea is unlike me, it has no time to sleep,
It always has a tide.
There is only one thing the same as me and the sea.
The sea and I have someone in charge.

**Joshua Bartlett (10)**
**SS Peter & Paul CE Primary School, Bexhill-on-Sea**

## The Seaside

Majestic waves crashing against the rocks
Tangy, salty air wafting up my nose
Laugher of children playing in the sea
Running my hand across the rigid shells
Soft ice cream tickling my taste buds.

**Victoria McDonnell (10)**
**SS Peter & Paul CE Primary School, Bexhill-on-Sea**

## Autumn

I see the autumn clearly blowing this way.
I can see the leaves blowing.
The wind is blowing through my hair so hard,
I feel like I am flying.

**Thida Streets (11)**
SS Peter & Paul CE Primary School, Bexhill-on-Sea

## What Am I?

Suspended like a silver ghost
I swing to and fro,
Pale and silver like
A polished snake.
Without a breeze my legs
Dangle dejectedly
And with wind I sound like
A thousand sleigh bells
Tinkling musically.
But in wind I jangle and
Crash.
I am as cold as ice
Like shimmering pipes
I swing in playgrounds,
Gardens and parks
Glimmering softly, majestic
And high.
Well, have you guessed
As I chime in the sky?
*What am I?*

Answer: wind chime.

**Leona Crawford (8)**
St Michael's Primary School, Withyham

## Rack Your Brains Riddle

Hard exterior
Orange and round
It's been growing all summer
On the ground

Pureed interior
With seeds really white
When Hallowe'en comes
It will give you a fright

You can carve it to scare
To fool and to trick
And the smell of it
Makes people feel rather sick

It looks so alive
With a tea light inside
Well, it's a . . .
I'll leave you to guess!

Answer: pumpkin.

**Charlotte Ashby (10)**
**St Michael's Primary School, Withyham**

## What Am I?

I sit in the corners of classrooms red and heavy,
Snoozing asleep,
Until the alarm clock wakes me from my slumber.
It's panic, confusion, excitement when I'm used!
A colossal pink alien from above strangles me to death
In the scorching heat
And makes me sick on the floor.
Then drops me crashing down below
And runs screeching out the door.

Answer: a fire extinguisher.

**Molly Deer (9)**
**St Michael's Primary School, Withyham**

## Guess What I Am

I lie dead by the trees in the forest,
Cold, wet and lonely.
All I am is bones.
I used to gallop happily
Before farmers shot me down!
People walk past me, ignoring me
Like I can't be seen anymore.
Now I lie in a deep, deep sleep,
Waiting and waiting.
All my light, white flesh gone,
Farmers take me away and eat me.
I wish they didn't shoot at me,
But I risked it for my family.
Can you guess what I am yet?

Answer: a deer skull.

**Wade Marais (8)**
**St Michael's Primary School, Withyham**

## What Am I?

I'm normally suspended in mid flight.
*Whoosh!* Dodge! Back and forth.
Unable to fly too far forwards or behind.
Just then I stop and everything stays,
Then the invisible beast races forward
In a flurry of movement moving me
And I break the silence.
I'm not too loud or quiet.
I have hollow tubes
Sometimes making eerie noises or nice clangs.
I'm sometimes made of metal or wood
But you can make me from scratch or I'm manufactured.

Answer: wind chimes.

**Kai Nelson (10)**
**St Michael's Primary School, Withyham**

# What Am I?

I am as round as an orange
And spin so fast I look like a blur.
You can find places around me
So I am very useful.
I stay in mostly homes and schools.
I am on a slight tilt and I am a model
Of something real.
I have lots of words on me
And I have very colourful skin.
I am as smooth as silk.
What am I?

Answer: globe.

**Luke Morgan (8)**
**St Michael's Primary School, Withyham**

# What Am I?

I can live in a glass box
I have a hard outer layer
I drink and eat there
Then I might grow
But if unsuccessful
I disappear into the undergrowth
I reproduce by spreading my insides
Out into the ground
I'm quite good for lots of things
Like food and fun on Hallowe'en.

Answer: a pumpkin.

**Samuel Hyde (10)**
**St Michael's Primary School, Withyham**

# Open The Door

Open the door and you will see . . .
Club penguin.
Open the door and you will see . . .
Winter sports shop.
Open the door and you will see . . .
The dock.
Open the door and you will see . . .
The forest.
Open the door and you will see . . .
My igloo.
Open the door and you will see . . .
The coffee shop.
Open the door and you will see . . .
The cave.
Open the door and you will see . . .
The mine.
Open the door and you will see . . .
Bunny Hill.
Open the door and you will see . . .
The iceberg.
Open the door and you will see . . .
A puzzle.
Open the door and you will see . . .
The book room.
Open the door and you will see . . .
The lighthouse and the beach.
Open the door and you will see . . .
The dojo.

Joe Lyons (7)
**St Pancras Catholic Primary School, Lewes**

# Open The Door . . .

Open the door and you will see . . .
A tiger brushing its silky fur.
Open the door and you will see . . .
A snake coiling around a tree.
Open the door and you will see . . .
A monkey swinging branch to branch.
Open the door and you will see . . .
A lion ready to pounce.
Open the door and you will see . . .
A hummingbird buzzing.
Open the door and you will see . . .
A bird squawking.
Open the door and you will see . . .
A turtle slowly moving.
Open the door and you will see . . .
An elephant stamping.

**Frankie Livesy Stephens (7)**
**St Pancras Catholic Primary School, Lewes**

# Medusa

There were no creatures in the wood . . .
Well, that's what we thought.
My blood went cold.
I heard a piercing scream,
I saw a green and black snake
Dead on the cobbled ground.
I saw a ripped, night-black cape on a branch,
I found a shining pearl-white tooth
With blood dripping from the jagged top,
I found a terrified, grey statue
Lying on the freezing rubble,
But his cold heart was still beating.
But we still didn't find . . . Medusa.

**Molly Osborne (10)**
**St Pancras Catholic Primary School, Lewes**

## The Zombie Dwarf

We didn't see zombie dwarves in the Lewes castle,
But what we knew was . . . they were there . . .

We saw skeleton bodies on the creaky floor,
With thick, old spiderwebs covering them.

We heard violent shouts down the misty corridor
And slow footsteps down the creaky stairs.

We discovered dead bodies in the secret chamber
With axes stuck in their necks
And daggers down their throats.

We smelt ancient blood on the deadly floor.
We found moving eyeballs in a cup of tea
And I felt a cold hand hold my shoulder behind me
And *crack!*
I'm knocked out.

**Sebastian Baynes (11)**
**St Pancras Catholic Primary School, Lewes**

# A TV Kennings

Primeval dodger
Soap watcher

Apprentice obsessed
Peppa Pig possessed

Movie screamer
Lottery dreamer

Documentary peeker
Comedy squeaker

Casualty excited
Jamie Oliver delighted

Family Guy looker
Advert for a cooker.

**Joe Windless (11)**
**St Pancras Catholic Primary School, Lewes**

# Vampires' Fort

There was evidence vampires were still here . . .
I saw blood crawling down on every wall,
I saw a black cloak floating,
As I reached out to grab hold of the handrail,
I felt something bloody,
Then when I looked, it was a heart still beating.
I saw rotting bodies with two holes in their necks,
I heard a bloodcurdling shriek,
A minute later a sucking noise.
I smelt burning flesh.
I saw a shadow with a cape.
I heard footsteps, it must be him.

**Miranda Costigan (11)**
**St Pancras Catholic Primary School, Lewes**

## Open The Door And You Will See

Open the door and you will see . . .
A film on TV.
Open the door and you will see . . .
A dragon having a wee.
Open the door and you will see . . .
A man showing his knee.
Open the door and you will see . . .
Some kiwi.
Open the door and you will see . . .
Only one pea.
Open the door and you will see . . .
Me!

Milton Thompson (7)
**St Pancras Catholic Primary School, Lewes**

## Vampires

We didn't see vampires
In the cold, freaky graveyard,
But we saw . . .
A vampire's black cloak
Fly by in the distance.
We found behind a gravestone,
A fresh piece of flesh.
We heard the most terrifying screams.
We discovered some rotting organs,
Nailed to the gravestone.
There was blood all over the cemetery floor
And still we didn't see any vampires.

Morgan Harris (10)
**St Pancras Catholic Primary School, Lewes**

## Mr Rarmus

Mr Rarmus, Mr Rarmus!
Please don't alarm us!
Please . . . you know your name.
Mr Hacefall, Mr Hacefall,
You really look disgraceful!
I never want to see you again.
Mr Vo, Mr Vo!
You are very slow.
Now . . . are you ready?
Mr Chell, Mr Chell!
What a nasty smell!
Tell me . . . where is my teddy?

Leon Reddick (7)
**St Pancras Catholic Primary School, Lewes**

## Bad Luck

I fell through a tree on the way to school
And I found myself in the land of dwarves,
Some of them green and some were tall.
Most of them were drunk.
I saw Gordon Brown dead in the mud
While I was playing blind man's buff.
I don't think I was happy,
But it's so hard to say go,
For nothing is what it seems
In the land of teen dwarves.

Luke Franco (10)
**St Pancras Catholic Primary School, Lewes**

## Dragons

Dragons, guess what I see?
A dragon coming straight for me.
Dragons, dragons, what do I see?
A dragon eating Harry Potter for his tea.
Dragons, dragons, what do we all see,
OMG - hide me!
Dragons, dragons, what do I see?
Oh, it's my mum calling me.
After a long day sweating head to toe,
It's time to play some tic tac toe.

Harrison Barton (7)
**St Pancras Catholic Primary School, Lewes**

## Ghosts

We could not see any ghosts in the graveyard,
But we did see objects floating in thin air.
We heard gravestones sliding to the side
To let out the ghosts.
We felt something zooming above our heads.
We smelt rotting bones, guts and flesh.
My heart almost jumped into my mouth.
I might not have seen ghosts in the graveyard,
But I saw the evidence that the ghosts are there.

Millie Brooks (9)
**St Pancras Catholic Primary School, Lewes**

## Untitled

You may not see black cats in a graveyard
But what I did see was the rotting flesh and bones
Of a decaying corpse,
Organs scattered across the ground
And blood trickling down the path beneath my feet.

Teige Dillon (10)
**St Pancras Catholic Primary School, Lewes**

# An Open Door

An open door is a new beginning,
An open door is a way out,
An open door can help you through
The times you want to scream and shout.

An open door is a new beginning,
An open door is a trusting friend,
An open door can help you find
That this is the beginning, not the end.

**Katerina Zoob (11)**
**St Pancras Catholic Primary School, Lewes**

# Cats In Carts!

Cats in carts, capes, carpets,
Capes on vampires.
Carrots, cucumber, cauliflower,
Carrots are for rabbits.
Clowns, crush, clouds,
Clowns make me laugh!
Tree, small, Paul, flea,
These don't begin with C!

**Camille Cooper (8)**
**St Pancras Catholic Primary School, Lewes**

# Vampire Death

We didn't see vampires in the castle
But we saw evidence.
We saw skulls on the floor,
We heard the hiss of a vampire.
I smelt the rotting flesh
And I saw a shadow.
It was the vampire.

**Henry Chown (9)**
**St Pancras Catholic Primary School, Lewes**

Poetry Explorers 2009 - Sussex

## The Banshee Of All Spirits

I never saw a banshee in the cave of spirits
But I knew it was there.
I saw the shine of silver tin foil.
The myrrh oil was still in the cracked bottle
With the shattered stopper.
I could still smell the scent of baking soda.
All had failed to catch her,
All would fall to . . . their death.

**Beatrix Livesy Stephens (9)**
**St Pancras Catholic Primary School, Lewes**

## Werewolves

You may not see werewolves in Werewolf Castle
But the signs are clear.
The bodies on the floor were drenched in blood.
The organs were rotting on the bloodstained floor.
The blood was dripping from the castle walls.
The petrifying screams echoed in the distance.
So now you know if anything goes *bump* in the night
Something is there . . .

**Alfie Crowley Rata (10)**
**St Pancras Catholic Primary School, Lewes**

## The Water World

Deep, deep down at the bottom of the sea,
There are people like you and me,
But they can swim with dolphins,
Turtles, whales and whale sharks too,
But the one they don't like is the sea monster who . . .
Has a very big nose, bigger than all of you.
When I look out to sea,
I wonder what there could be under that sea.

**Joel Penrose (7)**
**St Pancras Catholic Primary School, Lewes**

## Snow

Glistening snowflakes falling down quietly
Hitting the ground.
On the ground it's a carpet of snow.
Crunchy footprints wherever you go.
*Swish, swoosh,* through the snow,
Sledges sliding, off we go.
Crowds of people snug and warm,
Oh my gosh . . . *it's a snowstorm!*

**Evie Flynn (7)**
**St Pancras Catholic Primary School, Lewes**

## The River, Gliding Water

The water roared down the rocks
The trees slept soundly
The leaves parachuted down to the bank
The wind crept across the river
The grass slithered under my feet
The clouds shifted across the sky
The sun exploded with rays heating the ground.

**Alice Penrose (9)**
**St Pancras Catholic Primary School, Lewes**

## I'm Going To The Park

I'm going to the park.
I'm going to the park.
I'm going on the slide for a fun, fun ride.
I'm going on the swings, I feel like I have wings.
I'm going on the seesaw and I want more.
Now it's the end of a sunny, sunny day
And all I did was play, play, play.

**Zofia Galloway (7)**
**St Pancras Catholic Primary School, Lewes**

## Cats In Carts!

Capes on vampires
Carrots for rabbits
Cars to drive in
Clowns are scary
Cauliflower fluffy
Cabbages crunchy
All start with C!

Bailey Perrin (7)
**St Pancras Catholic Primary School, Lewes**

## The Ghost

I heard a ghost howling in the night sky.
I felt a cold chill running down my neck.
I saw the church's curtains fluttering.
I found a man that had been frightened to death.
I didn't see a ghost in the church
But I knew there was one in the mist of the night.

Fionn Lord (11)
**St Pancras Catholic Primary School, Lewes**

## The Cyclops

At first we didn't see one Cyclops in the dark, misty wood.
Then we saw massive, big Cyclops footprints
The size of an elephant's head.
Trees snapped down as if they were just flowers.
Scattered corpses with the flesh stripped from the bone.
The stink of swamp creatures in the air.

Jason Watson (9)
**St Pancras Catholic Primary School, Lewes**

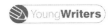

# The War Of Nature

The wind was laughing as it blew away the frightened leaves.
The dark clouds were stalking the bright sun.
The moon glared at the stars.
The trees were ducking the wind's icy blasts.
The rocks were knocking together in fright
And God looked on, as the world did its work.

Isaac Cowler (8)
**St Pancras Catholic Primary School, Lewes**

# Bees On Bears

Bees on bears
And bears on bicycles.
Bees that have birthdays,
Bees on bears
And bears on bicycles.
Bears that have bananas.

Phoebe Cullen (7)
**St Pancras Catholic Primary School, Lewes**

# Leaves

Leaves are smooth, dusty and damp.
They grow on trees.
Some are crunchy and some are pretty.
Some are scratchy on the ends.
There are all sorts of leaves.

Ellie Burall (7)
**St Pancras Catholic Primary School, Lewes**

## Pirates

Pirates, pirates, pretty Polly pirates
Pirates, pirates, pretty Polly, passion pirates
Pirates, pirates, pretty Polly, passion, pink pirates
Pirates, pirates, pretty Polly, passion, pink, parrot pirates.

Jessica Smith (8)
**St Pancras Catholic Primary School, Lewes**

## A Star

A star shining in the sky.
A star shining, I don't know why.
A star shining does not lie.
A star shining in the sky.

Saskia Vernon (10)
**St Pancras Catholic Primary School, Lewes**

## Seasons

Spring has blossom on the trees,
Lambs being born, leaves changing colour
And flowers coming up.

Summer, bees buzzing
And butterflies with amazing wings,
Multicoloured flowers everywhere,
The sound of laughter and the sun in the sky.

Autumn, conkers and acorns fall from the trees,
The orange, red and bronze leaves
Scattered on every path.
Walks in the wind and the sound of crunching on the ground.

Winter, gloves, hats and scarves,
Log fires and snow.
Rosy cheeks and smiling faces,
Holly and the robin's tune.

Matilda Taylor (10)
**St Philip's RC Primary School, Uckfield**

# What Happens In The Night

Charlie and Harry started to draw
Then it expanded into a war,
Stickmen, aliens and rock monsters too,
From spaceships to armies, they drew and drew.

Their armies grew bigger,
The fighting increased,
Only at bedtime,
The hostilities ceased.

All were asleep,
It was way past ten,
And out of the page,
Jumped the stickmen.

They stared at each other,
Weapons in hand,
'Are they asleep?'
Whispered Lieutenant Dan.

'All's clear!'
Cried General Kabam,
'Who's for a sandwich?
Ham or Spam?'

The creatures from the deep,
Got out the Scrabble,
Amongst the zombies
Arose a happy babble.

'They'll make us fight again tomorrow,'
Said the aliens wearily,
'But tomorrow night we'll play snooker!'
Responded the robots cheerily.

**Harry Cannon (10)**
**St Philip's RC Primary School, Uckfield**

## The Clown

Right in the centre of my town
There stood a very weird clown
He was dressed in all sorts of clothes
Then he did a mad sort of pose

That clown I swear
He's really not good
Doing his dance
In the neighbourhood

I thought to myself
What to do
And I looked out the window
He was on the loo!

I really couldn't
Believe my eyes
That clown he is
He's full of surprise

When I went
To my bed only last night
I could hear something
Something outside
Calling my name in the street light

In the morning the doorbell rang
It was my friend and she sang
'I got you, I got you, I got you yesterday
Didn't you know it was April fool's day?'

**Amy Batt (10)**
**St Philip's RC Primary School, Uckfield**

# Animals

Pigs, geese, cats or dogs,
Guinea pigs, fish and also
Hedgehogs!

Rabbits that hop wild and free,
Jellyfish and sharks that swim in the sea.

Pigs, geese, cats or dogs,
Guinea pigs, fish and also
Hedgehogs!

Mice that squeak, birds that squawk,
Even some animals that can actually talk.

Pigs, geese, cats or dogs,
Guinea pigs, fish and also
Hedgehogs!

Ducks that quack, donkeys that bray,
And some animals that like to play.

Pigs, geese, cats or dogs,
Guinea pigs, fish and also
Hedgehogs!

All kinds of animals that can be,
Even some that we can't ever see.

Pigs, geese, cats or dogs,
Guinea pigs, fish and also
Hedgehogs!

**Daisy-Anne Mayhew (10)**
**St Philip's RC Primary School, Uckfield**

Poetry Explorers 2009 - Sussex

## Alphabet Animals

A is for antelope who can jump very high
B is for birds that fly up in the sky
C is for cats that get stuck up a tree
D is for dolphins that swim in the sea
E is for elephants with great big, long trunks
F is for flamingos that despise smelly skunks
G is for giraffes that have very long necks
H is for herons, watch out for their pecks
I is for iguanas with sharp, spiny backs
J is for jackals who'll have you for a snack
K is for koalas all cuddly and grey
L is for llamas who like to eat hay
M is for meerkats who stand up straight and tall
N is for newts who are slimy and small
O is for otters who yap loudly all day
P is for puppies who have fun and play
Q is for quokkas who are quite small and fat
R is for rats what get eaten by cats
S is for snakes who slither and hiss
T is for tarantulas, they have got a killing kiss
U is for underwings who'll make sure your clothes are chewed
V is for vultures who scavenge for food
W is for weasels, lots of food they must scoff
X is for xanthias, that's Latin for moth
Y is for yaks, all big and hairy
Z is for zebras, stripy and wary.

James Sutton (11)
**St Philip's RC Primary School, Uckfield**

## My Hamster

I really love my hamster
She's a fluffy ball of fun
But I have to keep her in a cage
Or else she'll run, run, run!

Oliver Ellen (9)
**St Philip's RC Primary School, Uckfield**

# Christmas

Christmas Day, Christmas Day, I can't wait for Christmas Day,
Presents under the Christmas tree,
Just think how happy I will be.

Mince pies and carrots lined up on the fireplace
I would love to see Santa's face.

Holly on the banisters, ivy on the stairs,
Stockings on the fireplace hanging in pairs.

Night falls upon us as Christmas Day draws near,
I go to bed dreaming about the day that's nearly here.

Christmas Day is here, Christmas is here!
I pull back the curtains and the snow is also here!

I put on my warmest clothes and run down the stairs,
I pick up my welly boots which are lying on the chairs.

I go into the garden and get out my sledge,
Walking up the garden leaving footprints as I tread.

I jump on my sledge and down the garden I flee,
Unfortunately I end up in the hedge!

My brother and I have a snowball fight, I throw one with all my might,
He doesn't see it coming and it causes him a big fright!

Christmas Day is full of glee
And that's why I shout *whoopee!*

Sean Crozier (10)
**St Philip's RC Primary School, Uckfield**

# My Selection Of Transport

When I was young I had a trike,
When I was older I had a bike.
Then I had a supercar
And drifted like a superstar.
Now I have a motorbike.

Isaac Gauntlett (9)
**St Philip's RC Primary School, Uckfield**

## Seasons

Spring is warm with blossoming trees,
Daffodils nodding their heads in the breeze,
Lambs frolicking in the field,
Sheep protecting them like a shield.

Summer's hot with bright blue sky,
Aeroplanes flying by,
Flowers opening their little heads,
Standing in their flower beds.

Autumn's warm with a chill,
When the flowers stop and stand still,
All the leaves turn golden brown
And fall from the trees, blowing down.

Winter's cold with ice and snow,
Snowballs coming to and fro.
Snowflakes falling on the ground,
Without making a little sound.

**Bethany Lampard (10)**
**St Philip's RC Primary School, Uckfield**

## Bonfire Night

B onfire Night gives lots of light and delight
O ut in the cold
N obody's pets are in sight
F or they are not allowed out at this time of night
I n the flames the guy is wedged in tight
R emember he's who started this fight
E veryone must remember his might

N obody is without a fright
I n fact it is an awesome sight
G one are the fireworks into the night
H ot potatoes, hot sausages it is right
T onight is a perfect delight.

**Guy Beagley (11)**
**St Philip's RC Primary School, Uckfield**

# The Alien Rock Band

Upon a star, in a distant land
There lives an alien, rock and roll band
They jig to their music and they play to the crowd
They jump around singing stuff that's really, really *loud!*

One plays a solo and the crowd gives a roar
He starts playing louder and the crowd demands more
The band keeps on playing, putting the crowd in a trance
Then they jump off the stage and start to sing and dance.

At the end of the show the crowd goes wild
For the alien rock band called Nibble and Nile
The band walked outside and hopped in their rocket
With all their instruments plugged into their sockets.

Now, you haven't heard the last of the alien band
For they are playing on a beach in the very hot sand
But if you listen carefully you can still hear their sounds
Soaring across galaxies, echoing round and round.

**James Rushton (10)**
**St Philip's RC Primary School, Uckfield**


# Food

There's Stilton, Cheddar and blue cheese too,
If you eat them I don't know what will happen to you.
There's blue milk, green milk and red milk too,
If you drink it you may need the loo!
There's vanilla, chocolate and strawberry ice cream too,
If you eat it you may turn blue.
There's tomato, cheese and mushroom on pizza too,
If you eat it, it may taste like heaven or may taste like goo.
There's apples, pears and bananas too,
They are healthy and they are good for you.
There's carrots, potatoes and broccoli too.
There's loads of veg in store for you.

**Jessica Bond (9)**
**St Philip's RC Primary School, Uckfield**

## In The Beginning

At the very beginning, at the beginning of day,
God made up His mind and had to say,
'My world is getting too dark and dingy,
Let there be light, that's far less cringy.'
So light there was, but it was far too plain,
So much God had to say again,
'Now let there be sea and land,
As well, now that's not nearly, not nearly so bland.'
But God did not think it was quite enough,
So He created creatures, animals and stuff.
'It's nice to have creatures and stuff alike, but all the same,
Let's have some civilisation, those with brains.'
And that's how all us humans began,
Adam and Eve were the first who sang,
The historic songs still sung today,
Their history forgotten day by, day by day.

Grace Wood (10)
**St Philip's RC Primary School, Uckfield**

## Night Rescue

The waves are crashing on the sand
And all around is sea, not land.
The palm trees sway from side to side
And insects creep into their hides.
The sand is soft and hot to hold
Home to crabs and starfish, their colours bold.
I shudder now as evening creeps
Mosquitoes fly and frogs they leap.
My dinghy is tied up on the beach
I look for food, oh no, it's out of reach!
A far-off beam shines in the night
I shout and scream at the distant light.
Please hear my call and rescue me
As Mother cries, 'It's time for tea.'

Thomas Wasels (10)
**St Philip's RC Primary School, Uckfield**

## The Recycling Centre

The recycling centre is a busy place with
Lorries coming in and out collecting the waste.
*Smash, crash, smash* goes the glass and cans
As they enter the bins.
*Flop, slop* goes the paper and cardboard as
They go into the containers.
Squashed plastic tumbling into the bin.
People dumping wardrobes, desks, tables and
Chairs with a bang and a crash, split wood
Everywhere.
Cars coming in and out offloading the
Recycling into the various places.
Workers help people offload their waste and
Throw it into the bins around the centre.
Just another day for the workers and lorry
Drivers of the recycling centre.

**Thomas Rideout (10)**
**St Philip's RC Primary School, Uckfield**

## The Naras

Nara No 1 thinks she's cool
And she likes to think that she rules!

Nara No 2 is a sixthdruple loser
Plus everyone likes to sue her!

LaLa is the head girl
And she likes to buy a pearl!

Dipsa is her best mate
And she makes all the dorks late!

And then Gemini's the third
And loves to bully all the nerds!

So they are the Naras of the school.

**Ciara Gaughan (10)**
**St Philip's RC Primary School, Uckfield**

## When We Leave The House

When we leave the house
The footballs come alive
They play with the teddies
Who bounce and jump and dive.
When we leave the house
Paper turns to planes
They glide with pride
Above the Brio trains.
When we leave the house
The curtains swish
The light bulbs flash
And the music starts to play.
The TV turns on
And sings its daily song
For all we know
This happens every day.

Ronan Friel (10)
**St Philip's RC Primary School, Uckfield**

## Morning Daydream

Looking at the snowdrops falling off the trees
I'm trying to see what's hiding in the midnight breeze.
The midnight sky is as dark as ink
Owls hooting through the twinkling night.
The morning sunlight's glow is bright.
Snow is melting in the morn,
I am singing through the trees,
I seem to see the light of dawn
And feel the morning breeze.
Running through the waking sheep,
I come to a cliff and over I leap.
I find myself up high in the sky
And dream that I have wings to fly.

Kathleen O'Hara (10)
**St Philip's RC Primary School, Uckfield**

# The Old Man

There was an old man
Who lived on his own
His wife died 10 years ago
The cat is fat and has loads of bones
And that's the way his life goes.

There was an old man,
Who lived on his own,
He went on a train a long time ago,
He left his phone, don't ask me why,
A lady picked it up and went, 'Oh my, oh my!'

There was an old man
Who lived on his own,
His name was Santa Claus,
Ho, ho, ho.

**Georgina Andrews (9)**
**St Philip's RC Primary School, Uckfield**

# Seven Sorcerers

S is for seven people
E is for what they eat
V is for Venus
E is for their emotions
N is for never give up

S is for sound
O is for over the top
R is for running
C is for catch
E is for envy
R is for running faster
E is for environment
R is for running further
S is for scared stiff!

**Jessica Shrubbs (10)**
**St Philip's RC Primary School, Uckfield**

## Splash

If I had gills and a tail
I would touch the deep ocean blue.

If I had gills and a tail
I would taste the fish in the deep blue sea.

If I had gills and a tail
I would listen to roaring waves.

If I had gills and a tail
I would breathe the ocean blue.

If I had gills and a tail
I would gaze into the open sea.

If I had gills and a tail
I would dream in the sunset.

Alex Burgess (10)
**St Philip's RC Primary School, Uckfield**

## Peter The Crazy Trumpet Player

Peter got a trumpet for his birthday
He played it every day
Until his sister had had enough
And she ran away.

Peter took his trumpet to bed
It gave him a sore head
It got lodged in his ear
His mum could not get near.

At school next day what a surprise
He couldn't believe his eyes
There were trumpets all around
And they made a big sound.

Oliver McGibbon (9)
**St Philip's RC Primary School, Uckfield**

## School

School can be good,
School can be bad,
Make people happy,
Make people sad,
There are lots of sheets and work to do,
For you to wade your way through,
English, science, geography,
Maths, art and RE,
So if you're starting a new school,
Do not worry, just follow the rules,
For you won't be at school for long,
'Cause you'll be old, older, *older,* gone!

**Lauren Coates (10)**
**St Philip's RC Primary School, Uckfield**

## Hallowe'en

Ghouls and ghosts come out at night
Watch out or they'll give you a *fright!*
Witches and wizards cast their spell
Be very careful because some of them smell!
Carving pumpkins can be fun
They always make people run!
Vampires have very sharp teeth
Just like holly on a wreath
Graveyards are very creepy
Seeing the dead is very freaky
Hallowe'en is oh so scary
Not the time to be a fairy.

**Summer Ridgley (10)**
**St Philip's RC Primary School, Uckfield**

## Storm

Waves are shuddering, seagulls coming for their food
Sand blows to and fro
A storm is raging in the air
Lightning bolts hit the water
The water gets swept up by the wind
Then a cold silence
The sky turns blue
The sun beams through the world
The sailing boats emerge from the fog
The sky and sea are calm again.

**Phoebe Curran (10)**
**St Philip's RC Primary School, Uckfield**

## The Cool Classroom

Right little kiddies, go off and play
Until the fifth of May
Or maybe you would like to stay
And watch a little adult play
Maybe fake Superman will come in today
And give a little shiny tray
The classroom hamsters will love it
Or maybe they will have a fit
Today's the day when you can play
Until the fifth of May.

**Alexandra Saunders (9)**
**St Philip's RC Primary School, Uckfield**

## My Favourite Game

Football is fun
Because you get to run
Lots of nations
Play in different formations
Monday to Friday they will train
To play at the weekends in the sunshine and rain
Teams will attack and defend
To score more goals, so in the end
After all the fouls, teamwork, offsides and passing
The winning team will hear their fans chanting.

Callum Smith (10)
**St Philip's RC Primary School, Uckfield**

## Everything Is Lost

I've lost my head, I've lost my stool,
Whenever I sit down I always fall.

I've lost my feet, I've lost my legs,
And someone chucked me in a pile of pegs.

I've lost my hand, I've lost my arms,
Now I can't use a charm.

I've lost my body, there's no more to lose,
But now I am just a pile of clothes and shoes.

Alex Azzopardi (9)
**St Philip's RC Primary School, Uckfield**

## The Two Twins

I know these twins called Bib and Boo,
They have brown hair and their eyes are blue.

Their ears are big and their noses are small,
They are kind of in the shape of a ball.

Their teeth are square and their tongues are blue,
But their feet are normal like me and you.

They're weird I know, I agree with you,
But they are nice and kind to even their shoes.

Ellie Brigden (9)
**St Philip's RC Primary School, Uckfield**

## Hallowe'en Poem

H aunted
A *aarrrggghhh!* A vampire
L ights went out
L ots of scared people
O h and don't forget your scary-looking dad!
W icked witch
E *eeekkk!* A werewolf
E ven I was frightened
N obody survived, not even me so goodbye.

Ryan Bate (10)
**St Philip's RC Primary School, Uckfield**

## At Night

At night when everyone's asleep,
My teddies dance to the music beat.
Barbie dolls have a photo shoot
And my brother's train goes *toot, toot, toot!*
Batman comes and says, 'Do you like my cape?
I stuck it on with masking tape.'

Eve Friel (9)
**St Philip's RC Primary School, Uckfield**

# When Michael Eats Sponge Cake

When Michael eats sponge cake
Crumbs go on the floor
He flicks icing at his sister
Then he wants more.

Finn the dog likes cake
Some fell on his head
He likes eating icing
Better than bread.

**Michael Padwick (9)**
**St Philip's RC Primary School, Uckfield**

# Poems

Some are big
Some are small
Some are tiny
Some are tall

Some are happy
Some are sad
Some are good
Some are bad.

**Nirmal Rajasekaran (9)**
**St Philip's RC Primary School, Uckfield**

# Tickets

T here are lots of ways to buy tickets
I like collecting tickets
C onductors like to punch tickets
K ings have royal tickets
E veryone needs tickets
T ickets are marvellous things
S o how many tickets have you got?

**Thomas Wood (10)**
**St Philip's RC Primary School, Uckfield**

## Today I Saw . . .

Today I saw a little robin sitting on a hedge,
But then I rubbed my eyes and saw him standing on a ledge.
He was flicking through a newspaper whistling a merry tune,
Then in a flash he flew away, I hope he comes back soon.

Today I saw a squirrels scuttling on a tree,
But then I rubbed my eyes and saw him dancing with glee!
He had a pair of bagpipes and played a jolly song,
He vanished in a second, I hope he won't be long.

Charlie Martin (11)
**St Philip's RC Primary School, Uckfield**

## Fred

There is a little boy called Fred,
Who never gets out of bed.
His legs are made of spaghetti
And his head is made of bread.

And when he does a poo-poo,
He does it in his nap,
And when you go to change him,
You go, 'Pooh, what's that?'

Tabitha Reed (10)
**St Philip's RC Primary School, Uckfield**

## My Dad's Day

At the crack of dawn my dad wakes up with a yawn.
For breakfast my dad has tea and toast which he likes the most.
My dad gets in his car to go to work because it's very far.
When my dad gets to work he plugs in his wireless router into
his computer.
He has various things for lunch which he likes to munch.
My daddy has a long day and really wants to come home and play.

James Johnson (10)
**St Philip's RC Primary School, Uckfield**

## Scary Hairy

Dad, I need to know
Because it's getting scary
How you are so hairy
I talked to Mum
But she pinched my thumb
And said, 'Don't be dumb
If you're scared of him
Look at Mary.'

**Freddie Neill (10)**
**St Philip's RC Primary School, Uckfield**

## My Mouse

I have a small mouse,
So I made it a house.
It has a tiny head
And it sometimes plays dead.
It goes to bed at night
And wakes up in the light.
It is very fat,
To make it look cool I made it a hat.

**Jemima Beagley (9)**
**St Philip's RC Primary School, Uckfield**

## Chocolate

Chocolate, chocolate, it is so nice
It is much better than having lice
I could eat chocolate all day
But I might have a day off in May.
Easter and Christmas are the best times of year
Because we can eat chocolate till it comes out of our ears.
Chocolate, chocolate is so great
I think when we met I thought it was just fate.

**Dominic Rees (10)**
**St Philip's RC Primary School, Uckfield**

*Poetry Explorers 2009 - Sussex*

## Football

F ootball is fun, football is cool
O wen scored a goal, the crowd went wild
O ver the goal, nearly hit the crossbar
T ackling Rooney, down the pitch he goes!
B ut he goes for it wide again!
A big cheat, Chelsea score a goal
L it like the sun, the pitch shines
L ovely goal, England have won!

**Joseph Lower (9)**
**St Philip's RC Primary School, Uckfield**

## My Sister

My sister means the world to me and always will do.
When I hear her voice, it reminds me of a sweet,
never-ending melody.
Her love is like a peaceful river that flows right out to sea.
As the years go by, I think, *do I deserve such a joy as her?*
I pray with all my heart that she will forgive me
For all the wrongs that I have done to her.
My sister means the world to me and always will do.

**Beth Burchett (9)**
**St Philip's RC Primary School, Uckfield**

## Teachers Are . . .

T all people who work in schools
E ducation is their thing
A t break they all sneak in to get a
C up of tea
H orrible lessons they like doing best
E vil heads are horrific
R eading, writing and maths are torture
S orry to offend you, teachers.

**William Anderson (9)**
**St Philip's RC Primary School, Uckfield**

## Football

F ootball is fun
O n the field
O n the television
T errific goal
B alls kicked around
A referee
L arge crowds
L egs flying.

**Thomas Lowrie (9)**
**St Philip's RC Primary School, Uckfield**

## Friends Forever

F riends are special in different ways
R eliable, trustworthy with no delays
I will be her best friend, never her enemy
E nough to keep her company
N ever will we break up
D oes she like me or is she making it up
S he obviously does, so we are *best friends*.

**Millie Aldred (10)**
**St Philip's RC Primary School, Uckfield**

## Fairy Poem

'Mum, I saw a fairy,
Bright pink and small.
Her name is Isabella,
She works in fairy school.
I haven't had some chocolate,
I haven't had some sweets.
I think I just fell asleep.'

**Shauna Page (9)**
**St Philip's RC Primary School, Uckfield**

## Cheeky Cheese

The cheese is cheeky and very, very sneaky.
If you get in its way you'll turn into hay.
The cheese is cheeky and very, very freaky.
If you look close you'll see a ghost.
The cheese is cheeky and very, very geeky.
If he sees a man he will make a plan.

Adam Trueman (9)
**St Philip's RC Primary School, Uckfield**

## Bees

Bees, bees, they sting your knees,
And they live in colonies.
Bees, bees, they don't like cheese
And when they're dancing, they touch their knees!
Bees, bees, they make you sneeze,
When you ask, 'Honey please!'

James Allison (10)
**St Philip's RC Primary School, Uckfield**

## Homework Licence

Homework licence enables you
To tell the teacher what to do,
If you get one then you're able
To hog the whole dining table.
If you get one then you'll see,
That homework wasn't set out to be.
Look left and right and you will sight,
Your imagination taking flight
And you will imagine,
The teacher who set it,
Will suddenly,
Start to forget it!

Niamh McGuinness (11)
**St Robert Southwell Catholic Primary School, Horsham**

## Snow Trek

A frozen, desolate landscape,
Brittle, glassy, glinting ice.
Ground carpeted with snow,
Hiding treacherously thin ice.
Arctic wind biting at any uncovered skin,
Chilling and bitter.

Snow, soft and fluffy but cold,
Untrodden pathways and bare snow-laden trees.
Snowflakes floating down and burying land,
Transforming everything it falls on.
Glittering in deep, powdery snow banks,
Glistening and magical.

Caught in a blizzard,
Battered by hail, sleet and snow,
Snow muffling all sound apart from the piercing wind.
Sub zero temperatures,
Head down trudging through it.
Cold and icy.

An ice cave,
Sheltering but frosty,
Dazzling icicles hanging from the roof.
Slushy puddles slowly freezing.
Ice walls protecting from the blizzard.
Gleaming and shiny.

A new day and the blizzard has ended,
Trekking back to the cabin,
Where a warm fire and dry clothes await.
Back over now trodden ground.
Melting snow sticking to boots and sleeves.
Home again.

**Natasha Rogers (10)**
**St Robert Southwell Catholic Primary School, Horsham**

# My Dog Poem

I love my dog, he is so cute,
He is also sweeter than any fruit.
His fur is beautiful shades of black,
So nice that my eyes will never look back.
He also has massive blobs of white,
Looking splendid in the morning light.
When I come home he gives me a fright,
He jumps and jumps right to my head height,
Because he's so happy that I've come home,
So he won't be sealed in this dome alone.
My dog's name is Anakin, like in Star Wars,
It might be funny, but I wonder what's yours?
He is really fast and just a bit small,
And zooms around like a hairy cannonball.
He looks nice but sometimes he's mad,
Until into action comes my dad.
He eats as fast as a machine,
I sometimes can't believe his face isn't green.
His nose feels like a black jelly bean,
I hope he'll live longer than eighteen.
He has lots of friends when he goes outside,
He sometimes wishes that he could glide.
One time he ran right into our door
And the other he jumped to from floor to floor.
Here comes the end of my sweet doggy story,
Better hide it before my dog eats it in glory.

Ronnie Slowinski (10)
**St Robert Southwell Catholic Primary School, Horsham**

## My Beach

The blue, blue sky,
The blue, blue sea,
What a wonderful place to be.

As I surf,
As I splash,
The waves come tumbling,
All I hear is my tummy rumbling.

Great big waves,
On sunny days,
This is the place to be.

Great big dunes,
High up to the moon,
The sun shining,
My brother climbing,
What a wonderful place to be.

Barbecues boiling,
Everyone falling,
For the beautiful dinner tonight.

The sun is setting,
The sky is red,
And now it's time to go to bed.

Daniel Brydon (10)
**St Robert Southwell Catholic Primary School, Horsham**

## Summer

S ummer is fun, full of freedom,
U niversally, nobody is weary,
M illions enjoy the sizzling, fiery sun,
M ayhem on the beaches, laughter in the parks,
E ndless hours of boiling, blasting excitement,
R elax under the hot, burning sun.

Rachel Bowld (10)
**St Robert Southwell Catholic Primary School, Horsham**

*Poetry Explorers 2009 - Sussex*

## The Teddy Bear Picnic

When you're asleep, when you lay your head,
Your teddy bears slip out of their bed,
To a teddy bear picnic they wander away,
A whole lot of fun and a very good play.

Every teddy bear from afar,
Gather together at the teddy bazaar,
With teddy bear movies and decorations,
Lots of time put to make preparations.

The teddy bear children run around,
But when you wake not a mark will be found,
They'll pack away spic and span,
You may think not but the teddies can!

With toasted buns and freshly made cake
And you are just about to awake,
They rush back home to their neatly made bed
And you are just about to raise your head.

When they're asleep, when they lay their head,
We slip out of our neatly made bed.
So now you know our secret, keep it safe for now,
Don't tell anyone or you're just another moody cow!

Lucas Russell-Owers (9)
**St Robert Southwell Catholic Primary School, Horsham**

## Scorching Summer!

Summer, summer, beautiful summer,
Birds whistle in the trees,
Looking down at me,
Heat waves, beaches and lots more,
What about ice creams I adore,
Yum, yum, I want more,
Summer, summer, beautiful summer!

Erin Quinlivan (10)
**St Robert Southwell Catholic Primary School, Horsham**

## Under My Bed You Will Find . . .

Under my bed you will find . . .

A jack-in-the-box,
A handful of rocks,

A pot of gold,
Some dirty mould,

Frogs' eyes,
Undiscovered ties,

Lots of pies,
A few flies,

Ants that climb,
And look at the time,

And times tables on the wall,
Nothing very cool at all!

**Hayden Brock (9)**
**St Robert Southwell Catholic Primary School, Horsham**

## Running With The Ball

I'm running with the ball . . .

There's a big guy coming!
I quickly pass the ball to Paul.
He legs it to the try line.
He dodges right and left,
He's going very fast,
I don't know if he'll last.
He'll get tackled if he doesn't pass.
I run beside him, I'm calling for the ball.
I have it in my hands now,
I had better not fall.
I scored the try now, hooray!
I couldn't ask for a better day.

**Connor Howells (10)**
**St Robert Southwell Catholic Primary School, Horsham**

## My Tranquil Forest

My cat lingered for a while
Then he headed towards the forest.
I followed him into the forest.
Emerald leaves and dappled light
Gently tumbled onto the chocolate floor
And birds sang in harmony
With the soothing, soft sound of flowing water,
Where my cat stopped to drink
From the crystal, clear pool.
This forest seems so magical and enchanted now,
It's sunset and warm, gentle breeze rustling the leaves.
Now there is a soft glow of ruby-red, amber and saffron.
I think I'll stay here tonight in the light of the moon.
As the animals lull me to sleep, I say to myself,
*Goodnight magical world, goodnight, goodnight.*

**Isabelle Grant (10)**
**St Robert Southwell Catholic Primary School, Horsham**

## My Poem

My name is Dan the man
It is so fine it rhymes with
So many things, you just
Wait and see.

You know my name is
Dan the man, someone
Didn't like it so they
Chased me with a pan
And hit me with a can.

As you know my name,
You can go to the beach
With me and be a pain.
I am Dan the man
And I've got a tan.

**Daniel Longo (9)**
**St Robert Southwell Catholic Primary School, Horsham**

## The School Play

One day I came to school,
Then I went in the hall,
We all said,
As you know we have to flow,
So we put on a show
And you know we can glow
But not that well as you know
But we tried,
And it worked,
So now we have a mega flow
We were good
We were bad,
Now we can try again.

Quinn D'Arcy (10)
**St Robert Southwell Catholic Primary School, Horsham**

## Eight-Legged Hunter

Paused with patience, behind the thick, blond brambles,
Awaits the predator, greedy, fearless, gallant,
Brightly marked with metallic, shining colours,
Camouflaged like the tiger which is leaping,
Leaping, leaping . . .
Pounced on its prey, devouring the flesh!
Turned away, seeking more blood . . .

Sprinting in the deserted savannah,
No life in sight, anxious, alone, abandoned,
Tattered skin, bloodshot eyes,
Starving like a dying miracle, constantly fading,
Fading, fading away . . .

Caitlin Twell (10)
**Seymour Primary School**

## The Soldier

Hiding underneath the noisy battlements,
Devious, cunning, sly,
A strong, proud soldier covered head to toe in mud
And he's carrying a killer weapon in thick, gloved hands.
As alone as a minute plankton in the vast Pacific Ocean
And he's eagerly waiting,
Waiting, waiting.

Still silently waiting under the quiet battlements, too quiet,
Unseen, alone, unsafe, then
Suddenly the armoured target is spotted.
The spider pounces and the feeble enemy is falling,
Falling, falling.

Laiba Malik (10)
**Seymour Primary School**

## The Dancer And The Spy!

Dangling craftily in mid-air
Above the dark doorway,
Lurks a figure camouflaged cunningly,
A dark, shadowy figure!
It's as devious as a devil and it's
Stalking, stalking, stalking.

Pirouetting delicately in a dark,
Silent hall,
Leaps a talented figure out of the shadows,
A dancer with slim, smooth, flexible legs,
It's as bendy as a straw and it's
Spiralling, spiralling, spiralling.

Charlie Knott (10)
**Seymour Primary School**

# Gymnast Spider

Flexibly leaping elegantly through the air in a cheering circus,
Suspended, spiralling, spinning,
Her muscular body is strong and cunning,
Concentrating cleverly, like an agile hawk, expressing herself,
Twirling, twirling, twirling.

Anticipation building in the acrobatic circus,
Approaching mercilessly, a glint of evil in her eye,
Moving swiftly to the beat,
As delicate as a gymnast, but also as tough as a soldier,
She pounces, tearing apart limb from limb,
A shriek echoed through the air,
Devouring, devouring, devouring.

**Isma Saeed (10)**
**Seymour Primary School**

# Wolf Spider

Creeping sneakily in the deep, dark, doom-filled corner,
Waits a creature, loitering, hiding,
All in black, camouflaged in the door,
It's as big as the twin towers and it's hanging,
Hanging, hanging.

Turning swiftly on the stage,
Swirls an elegant creature,
Calm, clever,
Graceful, with long, black hair,
As flexible as an athlete,
It prances on its prey,
Killing, killing, killing.

**Dayna Ball (10)**
**Seymour Primary School**

## The Black Widow

The soldier dangles down from the heavy chopper,
Disguised, cunning, strong,
Twisting like a drill,
Camouflaging in the overgrown bushes,
Leaps a smart figure with extraordinary weapons and it's
Searching, searching, searching

Suspending delicately in mid-air in the dark night shadows
Shadowed, cunning, sneaky
Leaps a powerful figure with eight flexible legs
And it's clever as a spy
And it's killing, killing, killing.

Osman Zafar (10)
**Seymour Primary School**

## The Dancer

Moonwalking among the grass knots
Jumps a creature, athletic, muscly -
A spider with eight powerful, flexible legs, oh
It's graceful like a dancer, it's twirling
Twirling, twirling.

Not a web spinner
Which gracefully catches its dinner
Of bees which buzz and fly
But a twirling dancer
Who jumps down on its victim
As the swirling, turning dancer does.

Jeremie Jean (10)
**Seymour Primary School**

# Soldier

Attacking among the grass knots
Killing a creature quickly, sneakily
A spider with eight powerful, long legs, oh
It's as brave as a soldier and marching
Marching, marching

Not a web spinner
Which lies in for his dinner
Of beetles which scuttle and crawl
But a killer soldier
Who shoots down his victim
As the long lost soldier.

**Kurt Robinson (10)**
**Seymour Primary School**

# The Spider Gymnast

Dangling gracefully on a silken, threaded rope
In the quiet gymnasium,
Spinning, spiralling and suspended in mid-air,
A shadowed, powerful figure talented and creative,
She is as delicate as a snowflake and she's
Twisting, twisting, twisting.

Running slowly along to the vault in the gymnasium,
Dangling straight, still and secure,
Her pointed toes nearly reach the ceiling, as fragile as a vase,
But her hands are tense and she's waiting,
Waiting, waiting.

**Georgia Edwards (10)**
**Seymour Primary School**

## A Spider Gymnast

Running slowly to the pink vault in the damp studio,
Still, straight and suspended in mid-air,
Her pointed toes almost reached the ceiling, like the tallest woman
And she's waiting, waiting, waiting . . .
For the next performance on the next apparatus.

Hanging gracefully on the silken rope in the still studio,
Creative, talented and waiting in anticipation,
A powerful, shadowed figure silenced the crowd,
She was like a delicate leaf falling down
And then a furious, twisting tornado that leapt through the air
And she's spinning, spinning, spinning.

Iseoluwa Ojo (10)
**Seymour Primary School**

## The Spying Spider

Lurking upon the pure white ceiling
Pounces a little, terrifying creature dressed in black
A sneaky, little, evil thing which is waiting patiently
Oh God, it's as creepy as a wolf
And it's hanging, hanging, hanging.

Craftily hiding behind the door
Sneaks a black figure
A stalking, evil spider which is spying
Camouflaged like an insect in a pile of leaves
And it's as scary as a monster
And it's loitering, loitering, loitering!

Katie Kingshott (10)
**Seymour Primary School**

## The Policeman

Chasing among the streets
Arrests a creature punching, kicking
A police officer with two attacking, powerful legs, oh
It's huge as jail and it's pursuing
Pursuing, pursuing

Not a lazy policeman
Who waits in his car for his criminal
Or a bad guy who plans and runs
But a brave policeman
Who pursues the upset criminal
As the powerful policeman does.

**Brinley Elliott (10)**
**Seymour Primary School**

## The Spider

Sitting among the lakeside reeds
Strikes a creature, crafty, clever
A spider with eight strong, flexible legs, oh
It's as quiet as a fisherman
And it's waiting, waiting, waiting.
Not a web spinner
Which lies in wait for its dinner
Of beetles that struggle and pull
But a hungry fisherman
Who traps his prey
As the patient fisherman does.

**Ryan Gardener (10)**
**Seymour Primary School**

## The Gymnast

Skilfully twisting in the full auditorium,
Pirouetting like a tornado, energetic, artful,
Elegant legs straight and strong,
As flexible as a gymnast,
Twisting, twisting, twisting.

Flipping gracefully through the cold winter air,
Energetic, strong, flexible,
With long, flexible legs,
Rotating quickly like a roundabout,
Quickly, quickly, quickly devouring its prey.

Mark Stewart (10)
**Seymour Primary School**

## Terrifying Thief

Lurking sneakily in the dark night,
Camouflaged, silent and merciless,
A thief with a black hat and black clothes,
It's as cunning as a wolf and it's scattering,
Scattering, scattering.

Delicately coming out of the dark night,
Quickly, hurriedly, across the road,
Like a black panther with sharp, silvery claws,
Expertly flying in mid-air and it's killing,
Killing, killing.

Liam Spiers (10)
**Seymour Primary School**

## The Spider Thief

Lurking suspiciously among the deadly shadows
Creeps a camouflaged thief, silent, merciless
With a black bag dangling off its back
And it's as cunning as a panther and it's lingering
Lingering, lingering.

Travelling away from the bush
Tiptoes a thief shrouded and quiet
Hidden like a dark wolf
And it's as sly as a snake and it's biting
Biting, biting.

**Harry Philpott (10)**
**Seymour Primary School**

## The Spider!

Pirouetting on the crowded stage
Talented, artful, skilful
With long, thin, flexible legs
Rotating like a rusty roundabout in the lonely park
And it's walking, walking, walking.

Lurking around the whistling bushes
Sneaking suspiciously, a trapper
With dirty, hairy legs
Chasing like a furious hunter and it's
Crawling, crawling, crawling.

**Sanjidah Uddin (10)**
**Seymour Primary School**

## The Black Widow

Preparing its tools, in the operation theatre,
Waiting willingly, anxiously, patiently,
Ingeniously, seeing the patient with its enormous four pairs of eyes,
And it's as judicious as Frankenstein and it's coming,
Coming, coming!

Paralysing its prey, in the large surgeon's room,
Making incisions, injecting, dissecting,
Piercing flesh with its razor-sharp claws,
Slashing furiously, like a guillotine, and it's devouring,
Devouring, devouring!

**Haleema Faisal (10)**
**Seymour Primary School**

## The Spy

Lurking quietly amongst the vast, overgrown bushes,
Patient, cunning, crafty,
A figure with a terrifying, freaky mask,
It's as frightening as a wrestler and it's sneaking,
Sneaking, sneaking.

Dangling securely below a gigantic oak tree,
Hangs with hunger, hope and desire,
A figure with a creepy, jagged jacket,
It's as petrifying as a criminal and it's devouring,
Devouring, devouring.

**Akif Azeem (10)**
**Seymour Primary School**

## Soldier

Rolling among the grass knots
Communicates a creature, strong, fighting,
A spider with eight camouflaged, muscly legs, oh
It's brave as a lion and it's ordering,
Ordering, ordering.

Not a gymnast
That balances above its victim
Of snails which slide and crawl,
But a strong slider who fights for his dinner
As the shooting, strong soldier does.

**Harry Brooker (11)**
**Seymour Primary School**

## The Dancer

Twisting and twirling in the corner of the room,
Lurks a sneaky creature, fearless and vicious,
A spider with two sharp, fantastic fangs,
Spying cunningly, hung on a lacy web,
Like a Christmas decoration and it's
Looping, looping, looping.

**Ayesha Khan (10)**
**Seymour Primary School**

## The Spider

Flipping on the grass knots
Launches a creature, jumping, twisting
A spider with eight flexible legs
It's stretchy as a rubber band and it's
Twirling, twirling, twirling.

**Javed Malik (10)**
**Seymour Primary School**

## The Spider

Dancing serene across the spotlit stage,
Agile, elegant and graceful,
A beautiful ballerina,
Twirling delicately like autumn leaves and she is,
Pirouetting, pirouetting, pirouetting.

**Kayelah Siyar (10)**
**Seymour Primary School**

## The Seaside

Slow-moving clouds hover over the sea.
Transparent sea crashes down onto golden sand.
Bright, dazzling sand slips silently through your toes.
People swimming in freezing sea shiver all over as the day gets later.
Now the day is nearly over, the beach is bare
And a cold shiver falls over my back.

**Stephanie Baird (10)**
**Warninglid Primary School**

## Morning Mist

Ginger leaves in the tree blowing with the breeze
In the morning day is dawning in the summer sun
When the path is wet and soggy
Children have some fun
Magic mist moves mischievously when the day is done.

**Alice Burns (10)**
**Warninglid Primary School**

## Misty Woods

Never-ending trees as black as the night sky.
Bright, white mist is drifting slowly through the morning.
Shiny leaves begin to blow in the breeze.
Enormous branches gently hang over the path.
The cold path wiggles softly like a snake.

**Michael Hill (10)**
**Warninglid Primary School**

## The Castle

Dull clouds dancing and laughing.
Climbing castle calls for people.
Happy people enjoying the visit.
Flying flag flips and flaps.

**Curtis Malik (10)**
**Warninglid Primary School**

## The Hummingbird

The hummingbird swiftly catches its prey.
Flowers swish and sway, caught in the breeze
From the wings of the beautiful bird.
The dragonfly is trapped in the tip of the bird's beak.

**Cameron Martin (10)**
**Warninglid Primary School**

## The Eagle

Energetic river flowing very fast.
Hungry eagle hunting for fish.
Struggling fish fighting for freedom.
Water spray splashing up high.

**Harry Snell (10)**
**Warninglid Primary School**

*Poetry Explorers 2009 - Sussex*

## Bird Of Prey

Burning eyes are staring.
Water splashing cold.
Freckly fish is spinning to get free,
Bird's talons grabbing hard.

Ryan Fautley (11)
**Warninglid Primary School**

## Family

Family is home, wherever they are, you are
It's very simple, just like that!
They will always be there no matter what
They will always be there for you, even if you're not
It's very simple, just like that!
Family will make you laugh
It's very simple, just like that!
They will give you hugs
When you buy them memory mugs
Just to see them smile
It's very simple, just like that!
They will give you presents because they haven't seen you in a while
It's very simple, just like that!
Family will tell you the truth
Even if it drives you up the roof
It's very simple, just like that!
Family is the best thing that you can have
And they will always be there even if you can't see them
See, it's very simple . . .
Just . . . like . . . that!

Megan Baston-Steele (10)
**Westbourne House School**

# Battles

Screaming cries reach out at you like a rope
Pulling you to your death,
Red stains of blood like someone making wine with cherries,
Massive explosions as big as 50 elephants
Stacked one on each other.

Brave soldiers marching into their fate
Knowing that they might never see their family again.
Small children shivering in their homes
Waiting for their beloved father to come home.
The shiver of wind blowing the flags that wave in the wind.

The wives worrying about their husbands lying dead
Or maybe very badly injured.
Small snowflakes fall on the sea of dead bodies
Creating a soft blanket.

**Tara Noble (10)**
**Westbourne House School**

# What Did I Do Today?

On the way home from school, Ma asked me,
'What did you do today?'
I didn't really know the answers as I fell asleep in all seven classes,
So finally I plucked up the courage to lie and say . . .
'Did kung fu fighting in pyjamas with twelve sheep and eighty llamas,
Did geography in the pool, learnt skateboard tricks, mega cool!
Trained a twelve inch cow named Bart! Made paper aeroplanes
in art.
Played drums in music too, saw a whale on the loo.
Went on a plane to ancient Rome, met Julius Caesar,
then came home.'
Then my dear ma said to me,
'That's nice, dear, what would you like for tea?'

**Alice Jones (10)**
**Westbourne House School**

## Moonlight

Dazzling, glistening in the sky,
Shimmering far and wide,
Releasing a cosmic blanket
Wherever you will hide.

The shadowy bats surround its presence
Shining like the stars,
The late night larks covered in a lunar mist,
Glide across the surface.

The eclipse begins from light to dark,
Sending pulses through the sky,
The sun's solar power
Blinding all of life.

Dazzling, glistening in the sky,
Shimmering far and wide,
Releasing a cosmic blanket,
Wherever you will hide.

Moonlight.

Joshua Payne (11)
**West Park CE First & Middle School**

## The Goal

The concentration makes things a blur
The pressure, the determination
My heart's a drum
The tension, the accuracy
The ball flicks off my fingers
The fear and intensity
It circles the hoop, yes
The courage and power
Swish, it's in the goal
The cheer and the pride!

Rachel Hobden (11)
**West Park CE First & Middle School**

# Bang!

I feel the grip
In my feet,
And the power
In my legs,
My blood pumps
Quicker.

As my muscles
Stretch
And the feeling
In my mind
Harder and harder
To cope with.
*Bang!*
Here I go.

**Ossie Fish**
**West Park CE First & Middle School**

# The River

My eyes are stuck on the river,
As I squiggle out the mud,
Onto the flowing river,
The wind makes me quiver,
I row myself to the flag,
As I wait by the buoy,
Little birds come and go,
As I sit there all alone,
Waiting for the gun,
To start this race,
But my rival is not en route,
As he is taking up the flute,
I'm stuck here all alone,
Until my rival shows.

**Jessica Baker (11)**
**West Park CE First & Middle School**

*Poetry Explorers 2009 - Sussex*

# When I Go Swimming

When I go swimming,
I get the feeling
That I'm going to drown,
So I feel like a clown.

I stepped down that step
And on my head,
My swimming hat kept,
Both my hat and costume are red.

When I dive,
My goggles come off,
Oh, how I cried
When my goggles came off.

Maisie Clilverd-Buss & Leah Barnes (10)
**West Park CE First & Middle School**

# My Hero

Leona is my hero
And I'll tell you why.
When I hear her singing,
My eyes start to cry.
Her strong, tuned voice,
Above the rest,
I'm glad she won 'cause
She's the best.
Her singing flows out,
Like the open shore,
With the sunset above
And the world pleading for more.

Amber Hamilton (11)
**West Park CE First & Middle School**

## Watching And Waiting

I sit next to Dad,
Watching and waiting,
I sit on Mum's lap,
Watching and waiting,
I sit in my seat,
Watching and waiting,
I sit intensely,
Watching and waiting,
I sit and watch until . . .
*Splash!*

Molly Vigor
**West Park CE First & Middle School**

## Game, Set And Match

I have the ball in one hand,
The racket in the other.
I release the ball upwards
And swing the racket to meet it.

The ball flies rapidly towards the net,
A quiet prayer in my head . . .

Helen Skingley (11)
**West Park CE First & Middle School**

## My Heroine

She washes my clothes
She does my hair
She makes everything seem so fair
I love her so much
Because she is my mum
Together we equal just one.

Thea Langley (10)
**West Park CE First & Middle School**

## My Special Senses

Such a beautiful sight I saw:
Trees dancing in the light breeze,
Gently forcing through the air,
Making me calm lying in my bed,
Such a sight I saw.

Such a sensational smell I smelt:
A turkey roasting,
On a cold Christmas Day,
Memories of how it melts in my mouth,
Such a smell I smelt.

Such a sound I heard:
Baby birds calling their mothers,
Then singing together,
Memories of relaxing summer days in the garden,
Such a sound I heard.

Such a taste I tasted:
Freshly baked bread,
With butter spread on top,
It reminds me of baking with my mum,
Such a taste I tasted.

Such a soft touch I felt:
As my pet slept on my lap,
Not gritty or sweaty but silky soft,
Reminding me of peaceful nights,
Such a touch I felt.

**Katie Chadburn (11)**
**Whitehawk Primary School**

# The Magic Senses

Such a sight I saw
The blue sea roaring
Crashing on the shore
It lifted my spirits high
Such a sight I saw

Such a sound I heard
The trees swaying
On the green hills
It made me want to dance
Such a sound I heard

Such a smell I smelt
The soft roses
In many different colours
Their calming scent floated around in the air
Such a smell I smelt

Such a taste I tasted
Hot roast dinner
Juicy carrots too
Melting in my mouth
Such a taste I tasted

Such fur I felt
Soft, cuddly fur
As my rabbit sleeps on my lap
It made me feel sleepy
Such fur I felt.

**Lucy Hellier (10)**
**Whitehawk Primary School**

# My Five Magical Senses

Such a sight I saw:
A blue, cold, wavy sea
As calm as a wavy bee
A streaming flow of water
Such a sight I saw.

Such a sound I heard:
A honk from a car
As I'm passing by
A drop of rain falls
Such a sound I heard.

Such a smell I smelt:
The smell of flowers
As I'm walking by
Breathing through my nose
Such a smell I smelt.

Such a fur I felt:
As I lay cosily
With my cat on my lap
Stroking the softness of her fur
Such a fur I felt.

Such a taste I tasted
The softness of melted chocolate
It hits my mouth and starts to trickle through my throat
Such a taste I tasted.

**Danielle Harrington (10)**
**Whitehawk Primary School**

# The Senses

Such a sight I saw:
A tree dancing in the wind
Children's hair blowing in the wind
I shiver in the cold wind
As it bites my finger.
Such a sight I saw:

Such a taste I tasted:
Piece of delicious apple pie
Slowly tasting it to make it last.
Such a taste I tasted.

Such a smell I smelt:
A blueberry pie coming to my nose.
A lovely chocolate ice cream I smelt,
It smelt like lovely chocolate by itself.
Such a smell I smelt.

Such a noise I heard:
Birds singing on the tree like famous singers,
They sang their song slowly.
Such a noise I heard.

Such a thing I felt:
A spider crawling up my arm.
Drips of water drops on my arm
And my mum holding my hand.
Such a thing I felt.

**Zoe Vanhinsbergh (10)**
**Whitehawk Primary School**

# The Five Magic Senses

Such a sight I saw
Trees swaying in the breeze
Golden leaves shining in the sun
They make me want to dance
Such a sight I saw

Such a smell I smelt
Bread rising in the oven
Mmm, I can smell it now
Memories of when I first baked cakes
Such a smell I smelt

Such a sound I heard
Branches scratched at the window
I feel all shaky inside
I can remember when one of the branches hit our car
Such a sound I heard

Such a taste I tasted
The delicious icing hit my mouth
I couldn't stop eating them as it melted in my mouth
Such a taste I tasted

Such a touch I felt
My soft, furry cat sleeps on my lap
It is soft and cuddly as my teddy
Such a touch I felt.

**Lauren Stenning (11)**
**Whitehawk Primary School**

# Senses

Such a sound I heard,
The twittering of birds in the sky,
Fluttering of wings beating high,
As the sound slowly calmed down,
Such a sound I heard.

Such food I tasted,
Meatloaf and pie lying on my tongue,
The warmness pierced through my body
And then it changed,
Blueberry pie and whipped cream,
Such food I tasted.

Such a sight I saw,
The sun glistening in the sky,
The warmth lingered on my body,
Soon the sunset painted the sky,
Such a sight I saw.

Such fur I felt,
The warmth of fur slept on my lap,
It moved to get comfortable,
Almost fell but I caught it,
His tail brushed my face,
Such fur I felt.

**Owen Curd (11)**
**Whitehawk Primary School**

## The Magic Sense

Such a sight I saw:
Trees swaying side to side,
It makes me want to dance.
Such a sight I saw.

Such a sound I heard:
Birds singing in the trees,
It makes me want to sing.
Such a sound I heard.

Such a smell I smelt:
As the scent of the flowers in the wind
Mixed with soft roses
It reminded me of my own world.
Such a smell I smelt.

Such a touch I felt:
As the silky, smooth, soft roses blows into my face
It reminds me of a garden with lots of flowers and roses.
Such a touch I felt.

Such a tasty taste I tasted:
As the sweet tea hides my tongue,
It reminds me of a chocolate cake.
Such a tasty taste I tasted.

**Sophie Costen (10)**
**Whitehawk Primary School**

# My Five Magical Senses

Such a sight I saw
Trees up high moving side to side
The golden sand sparkling in my eyes
Shells on the beach make me want to touch
Such a sight I saw

Such a sound I heard
Leaves rustling crunch when I step on them
Such a sound I heard

Such a smell I smelt
The golden turkey cooking
The new loaf of bread
The scented rose freshly picked from the garden
Such a smell I smelt

Such a taste I tasted
The smooth gravy perfect with a roast
My tongue melts when I take the first bite
Of home-made curry

Such a touch I felt
The warmth of hot chocolate
The fur of the kitten like a furry ball
Such a touch I felt.

**Katana Linley (10)**
**Whitehawk Primary School**

## My Four Magic Senses

Such a sight I saw:

A sunset bursting through the clouds
Like the missed colours of the rainbow
I'm on the clouds watching seagulls flying by
Such a sight I saw:

Such a sound I heard:

My ears are full of calmness
Waterfalls splashing onto the rocks
Making a tapping sound
Such a sound I heard:

Such good food I tasted:

The mixture of peppers and curry
As hot as the sun
Such good food I tasted:

Such breeze I felt:

The cool breeze makes the leaves fly high
Leaving withered leaves
Scattered around my feet
Such breeze I felt.

**Maisie Wheeler (10)**
**Whitehawk Primary School**

# Five Senses

Such a sight I saw
A fish with shark teeth
And a dolphin tail
Such a sight I saw

Such a smell I smelt
A rose that smelt like a piece of rotting cheese
Such a smell I smelt

Such a sound I heard
A bit like a rocket going to the moon
And coming back from the moon
Such a sound I heard

Such a taste I tasted
A piece of rotting cheese
It had smoke coming out of it
Such a taste I tasted

Such a touch I touched
A meaty thing I touch
That makes your hand rot
Such a touch I touched.

**Leigh Adams (10)**
**Whitehawk Primary School**

Poetry Explorers 2009 - Sussex

# Young Writers Information

We hope you have enjoyed reading this book - and that you will continue to enjoy it in the coming years.

If you like reading and writing poetry drop us a line, or give us a call, and we'll send you a free information pack.

Alternatively if you would like to order further copies of this book or any of our other titles, then please give us a call or log onto our website at www.youngwriters.co.uk.

Young Writers Information
Remus House
Coltsfoot Drive
Peterborough
PE2 9JX
(01733) 890066